Praise for Nora Ephron

"Her finely honed wit is as fresh as ever." —*People*
"Nora Ephron has become timeless."
—*Los Angeles Times*
"A wickedly witty and astute writer." —*Boston Globe*
"Wry and amusing . . . Marvelous."
—*Washington Post Book World*

ALSO BY NORA EPHRON

FICTION

Heartburn

ESSAYS

I Feel Bad About My Neck
Scribble Scribble
Crazy Salad

DRAMA

Imaginary Friends

SCREENPLAYS

Bewitched (with Delia Ephron)
Hanging Up (with Delia Ephron)
You've Got Mail (with Delia Ephron)
Michael (with Jim Quinlan, Pete Dexter, and Delia Ephron)
Mixed Nuts (with Delia Ephron)
Sleepless in Seattle (with David S. Ward and Jeff Arch)
This Is My Life (with Delia Ephron)
My Blue Heaven
When Harry Met Sally . . .
Cookie (with Alice Arlen)
Heartburn
Silkwood (with Alice Arlen)

Wallflower at the ORGY

Nora Ephron

BANTAM BOOKS

WALLFLOWER AT THE ORGY
A Bantam Book / published by arrangement with the author

PUBLISHING HISTORY
Viking edition published October 1970
Bantam edition / July 1980
Bantam trade paperback reissue / July 2007

These stories originally appeared in *Esquire, Cosmopolitan, Eye, Holiday, New York,*
the *New York Times Book Review,* and the *New York Times Magazine* in slightly different form. "If You're a Little Mouseburger, Come With Me. I Was a Mouseburger
And I Will Help You." originally appeared in *Esquire* under the title "Helen Gurley
Brown Only Wants to Help."

Published by
Bantam Dell
A Division of Random House, Inc.
New York, New York

All rights reserved
Copyright © 1967, 1968, 1969, 1970, 1971 by Nora Ephron
Introduction © 1980 by Nora Ephron
Cover art copyright © 2007 by High Design

Book design by Glen M. Edelstein

Library of Congress Catalog Card Number: 73125948

Bantam Books and the rooster colophon are registered trademarks of Random
House, Inc.

ISBN 978-0-553-38505-2

Printed in the United States of America
Published simultaneously in Canada

www.bantamdell.com

BVG 10 9 8 7 6 5 4 3 2 1

THIS BOOK IS FOR DAN

Contents

Preface to the 1980 Edition

WALLFLOWER AT THE ORGY, my first collection, was published in 1970. It contains the first group of articles I sold to magazines after I left the *New York Post*, where I was a reporter for five years. I don't think anything could have better prepared me for magazine writing than those years at the *Post*—though not for the reasons you might suspect. The *Post* was a terrible newspaper in the era I worked there, and everyone knew it: as a result, those of us who worked for the *Post* were treated far more shabbily than reporters for other newspapers. It was often extremely difficult to get an interview with whomever you were writing about; and if you did get an interview, it often took place at the end of the day, after the subject was exhausted from hours of interviews with reporters from more important media outlets. I remember, in my years at the *Post*, reading the Arts and Leisure section of the Sunday *New York Times* and wondering why the reporters for that section were able to spend entire days with subjects I could barely get in to see; it never crossed my mind that it might have more to do with the clout of the publication involved than with the charm of the reporter. But the point is this: I was better off with my forty-five minutes because I was forced to report *around* the subject. I learned to go through the clips, find the names of people from the subject's past, hunt them up in old telephone books, track them down, and pull out anecdotes they knew. What I'm saying may seem obvious; but one of the things that stuns me is how seldom reporters do this: the standard magazine profile these days seems to be written after a reporter spends a lot of time with the person the profile's about, and only with that person. I can't imagine that. I can't imagine even going to see the person the profile's about until I've seen twenty or thirty people who knew him when.

The other advantage to all those years in the newspaper business is that I learned to write short. Much too short probably, but as vices go, that's far better than much too long. Nothing in the *Post* ran over fifteen hundred words: six hundred words was more like it. And the lack of space forced me to select, to throw out everything but the quote I liked best, the story that seemed most telling. Again, I don't mean to sound obvious, but several years ago I spent a year as a magazine editor, and I realized how difficult selectivity is for reporters who are spoiled by large amounts of space. I also don't mean to sound as if I learned all this on my own; I had good editors at the *Post*. I complained about them at the time, complained as they slashed out what I thought of as my gorgeous stylistic flourishes and what they thought of as wretched excesses largely inspired by worship of Tom Wolfe. But they were right. And as a result, my writing style—such as it is—is very spare. Which is lucky for me, because it turned out that there were very few editors in the magazine business as good as those I had at the *Post*.

Because I began as a newspaper reporter, it took me a long time to become comfortable using the first-person singular pronoun in my work. In the articles in this book I used it gingerly, often after considerable prodding from my editors. I was uncomfortable with it. The work I have done subsequently is considerably more personal and considerably more full of the first-person singular pronoun, but I still believe that the best approach to its use ought to be discomfort. Do you really need it? Does it add something special to the piece? Is what you think interesting enough to make the reader care? Are you saying something that no one has said? Above all, do you understand that you are not as important as what you're covering? We are now in an era when the I-lost-my-laundry-while-covering-Yalta school of reporting has become an epidemic; when serious books that involve reporting often tend to be suffused with the author's admiration of his own investigative techniques; when the narcissism of the press almost outstrips the narcissism elsewhere in the country. *The image of the journalist as wallflower at the orgy has been replaced by the journalist as the life of the party.* I look back on the original introduction to this book with a nostalgia that borders on pain. "There are times when I am seized with an almost uncontrollable desire to blurt out, in the middle of interviews, 'Me! Me! Me! Enough about *you*. What about *me*?' " I actually wrote that. I actually believed that. And now, here I am, after two subsequent books—and the book tours, the newspaper interviews, the television talk shows, after all the me-me-me. "It must be difficult being on the other side of the notebook," the reporters who interview me say. No. Not particularly. It's boring. And unbelievably repetitive. And terminally narcissistic. But not difficult.

Rereading this collection produced other fits of nostalgia. I am no longer the young woman who wrote about being made over by *Cosmopolitan* magazine, and I am no longer interested enough in the culture of kitsch to defend Jacqueline Susann. But here are these remnants of my former self, old snakeskins, and it amuses me to read them and remember how dippy I used to be. There are also pieces here that I'm proud of. But there's nothing here extraordinary or brilliant; I am a journeyman, and if these articles work, they work as examples of old-fashioned journalism. I am not a new journalist, whatever that is; I just sit here at the typewriter and bang away at the old forms. Which is fine with me.

Introduction

Some years ago, the man I am married to told me he had always had a mad desire to go to an orgy. Why on earth, I asked. Why not, he said. Because, I replied, it would be just like the dances at the YMCA I went to in the seventh grade—only instead of people walking past me and rejecting me, they would be stepping over my naked body and rejecting me. The image made no impression at all on my husband. But it has stayed with me—albeit in another context. Because working as a journalist is exactly like being the wallflower at the orgy. I always seem to find myself at a perfectly wonderful event where everyone else is having a marvelous time, laughing merrily, eating, drinking, having sex in the back room, and I am standing on the side taking notes on it all.

I am not, I must tell you, entirely happy with this role. There are times when I would much prefer to be the one having the fun; there are times when I am seized with an almost

uncontrollable desire to blurt out, in the middle of interviews, "*Me! Me! Me!* Enough about *you*. What about *me?*" But
then I remember that, like so many journalists, I am stuck on
the sidelines not just because I happen to be making a living
at the job but because of the kind of person I am and the reason I was drawn to this business.

Everyone I know who writes has an explanation for it,
and for years I went around collecting them, hoping that
someone else's reason would turn out to be mine. The first
person who gave me what seemed like a good one was a col-
league on the *New York Post* (where I worked for five years),
who told me during my first week there that the reason she
loved her work was that every day, on the way home from
work, she could see people on the subway reading her articles. For four years I looked around the subway to find someone reading mine. No one ever was. And finally, one day, it
happened: the man next to me opened to a story of mine,
folded the paper carefully back to settle in for a long read,
and began. It took him exactly twenty seconds to lose interest, carefully unfold the paper, and turn the page.

Then I remember asking a man who had no real reason
for working at a daily newspaper why he was there. "I'll tell
you," he said. "I can't think of any place I would rather have
been the day the President was killed than in a newspaper
office." And that seemed like a wonderful reason—and I
thought of the day President Kennedy was shot and the per-
verse sense of pleasure I got from working under deadline
that day, the gratitude for being able to write rather than
think about what had happened, the odd illusion of somehow being on top of the situation.

But in the end, the reason I write became quite obvious
to me—and it turned out to have much more to do with

temperament than motivation. People who are drawn to journalism are usually people who, because of their cynicism or emotional detachment or reserve or whatever, are incapable of being anything but witnesses to events. Something prevents them from becoming involved, committed, and allows them to remain separate. What separates me from what I write about is, I suspect, a sense of the absurd that makes it difficult for me to take many things terribly seriously. I'm not talking about objectivity here (I don't believe in it), nor am I saying that this separateness makes it impossible to write personal journalism. I always have an opinion about the orgy; I'm just not down on the floor with the rest of the bodies.

I feel that I should tell you a little about myself before letting the book begin. I feel this largely because I have just read the introductions to nine other collections of magazine articles, and all of them are filled with juicy little morsels about the people who wrote them. I think, however, that there is quite enough of me in most of these articles for me to forgo telling you how I love eating McIntosh apples and Kraft caramels simultaneously. That kind of thing. I should say that almost everything in this book was written in 1968 and 1969, and almost everything in it is about what I like to think of as frivolous things. Fashion, trashy books, show business, food. I could call these subjects Popular Culture, but I like writing about them so much that I hate to think they have to be justified in this way—or at least I'm sorry if they do.

One night not too long ago I was on a radio show talking about an article I had written for *Esquire* on Helen Gurley Brown and I was interrupted by another guest, a folk singer, who had just finished a twenty-five-minute lecture on the need for peace. "I can't believe we're talking about Helen

Gurley Brown," he said, "when there's a war going on in Vietnam." Well, I care that there's a war in Indochina, and I demonstrate against it; and I care that there's a women's liberation movement, and I demonstrate for it. But I also go to the movies incessantly, and have my hair done once a week, and cook dinner every night, and spend hours in front of the mirror trying to make my eyes look symmetrical, and I care about those things, too. Much of my life goes irrelevantly on, in spite of larger events. I suppose that has something to do with my hopelessly midcult nature, and something to do with my Hollywood childhood. But all that, as the man said, is a story for another time.

New York, May 1970

Wallflower
at the
Orgy

The Food Establishment:

Life in the Land of the Rising Soufflé
(Or Is It the Rising Meringue?)

One day, I awoke having had my first in a long series of food anxiety dreams (the way it goes is this: there are eight people coming to dinner in twenty minutes, and I am in an utter panic because I have forgotten to buy the food, plan the menu, set the table, clean the house, and the supermarket is closed). I knew that I had become a victim of the dreaded food obsession syndrome and would have to do something about it. This article is what I did.

Incidentally, I anticipated that my interviews on this would be sublime gourmet experiences, with each of my subjects forcing little goodies down my throat. But no. All I got from over twenty interviews were two raw potatoes that were guaranteed by their owner (who kept them in a special burlap bag on her terrace) to be the only potatoes worth eating in all the

*world. Perhaps they were. I don't know, though; they
tasted exactly like the other potatoes I've had in
my life.*

September 1968

You might have thought they'd have been polite enough not
to mention it at all. Or that they'd wait at least until they got
through the reception line before starting to discuss it. Or
that they'd hold off at least until after they had tasted the
food—four tables of it, spread about the four corners of
the Four Seasons—and gotten drinks in hand. But people
in the Food Establishment are not noted for their manners
or their patience, particularly when there is fresh gossip. And
none of them had come to the party because of the food.

They had come, most of them, because they were associated with the Time-Life Cookbooks, a massive, high-budget
venture that has managed to involve nearly everyone who is
anyone in the food world. Julia Child was a consultant on
the first book. And James Beard had signed on to another.
And Paula Peck, who bakes. And Nika Hazelton, who reviews cookbooks for the *New York Times Book Review*. And
M. F. K. Fisher, usually of *The New Yorker*. And Waverley
Root of Paris, France. And Pierre Franey, the former chef of
Le Pavillon who is now head chef at Howard Johnson's. And
in charge of it all, Michael Field, the birdlike, bespectacled,
frenzied gourmet cook and cookbook writer, who stood in
the reception line where everyone was beginning to discuss
it. Michael was a wreck. A wreck, a wreck, a wreck, as he
himself might have put it. Just that morning, the very morn-

ing of the party, Craig Claiborne of the *New York Times*, who had told the Time-Life people he would not be a consultant for their cookbooks even if they paid him a hundred thousand dollars, had ripped the first Time-Life cookbook to shreds and tatters. *Merde alors*, as Craig himself might have put it, how that man did rip that book to shreds and tatters. He said that the recipes, which were supposed to represent the best of French provincial cooking, were not even provincial. He said that everyone connected with the venture ought to be ashamed of himself. He was rumored to be going about town telling everyone that the picture of the soufflé on the front of the cookbook was not even a soufflé—it was a meringue! *Merde alors!* He attacked Julia Child, the hitherto unknockable. He referred to Field, who runs a cooking school and is author of two cookbooks, merely as a "former piano player." Not that Field wasn't a former piano player. But actually identifying him as one—*well!* "As far as Craig and I are concerned," Field was saying as the reception line went on, "the gauntlet is down." And worst of all—or at least it seemed worst of all that day—Craig had chosen the day of the party for his review. Poor Michael. How simply frightful! How humiliating! How delightful! "Why did he have to do it today?" moaned Field to Claiborne's close friend, chef Pierre Franey. "Why? Why? Why?"

Why indeed?

The theories ranged from Gothic to Byzantine. Those given to the historical perspective said that Craig had never had much respect for Michael, and they traced the beginnings of the rift back to 1965, when Claiborne had gone to a restaurant Field was running in East Hampton and given it *one* measly star. Perhaps, said some. But why include Julia in the blast? Craig had done that, came the reply, because he had never liked Michael and wanted to tell Julia to get out of Field's den of thieves. Perhaps, said still others. But mightn't he also have done it because his friend Franey had signed on as a consultant to the *Time-Life Cookbook of Haute Cuisine* just a few weeks before, and Craig wanted to tell *him* to get out of that den of thieves? Perhaps, said others. But it might be even more complicated. Perhaps Craig had done it because he was furious at Michael Field's terrible review in the *New York Review of Books* of Gloria Bley Miller's *The Thousand Recipe Chinese Cookbook*, which Craig had praised in the *Times*.

Now, while all this was becoming more and more arcane, there were a few who secretly believed that Craig had done the deed because the Time-Life cookbook was as awful as he thought it was. But most of those people were not in the Food Establishment. Things in the Food Establishment are rarely explained that simply. They are never what they seem. People who seem to be friends are not. People who admire each other call each other Old Lemonface and Cranky Craig behind backs. People who tell you they love Julia Child will add in the next breath that of course her husband *is* a Republican and her orange Bavarian cream recipe just doesn't work. People who tell you Craig Claiborne is a genius will insist he had little or nothing to do with the *New York Times Cookbook*, which bears his name. People will tell you that Michael Field is delightful but that some people do not take success quite as well as they might. People who claim that Dione Lucas is the most brilliant food technician of all time further claim that when she puts everything together it comes out tasting bland. People who love Paula Peck will go on to tell you—but let one of *them* tell you. "I love Paula," one of them is saying, "but *no* one, absolutely *no* one understands what it is between Paula and monosodium glutamate."

Bitchy? Gossipy? Devious?

"It's a world of self-generating hysteria," says Nika Hazelton. And those who say the food world is no more ingrown than the theater world and the music world are wrong. The food world is smaller. Much more self-involved. And people in the theater and in music are part of a culture that has been popularly accepted for centuries; people in the food world are riding the crest of a trend that began less than twenty years ago.

In the beginning, just about the time the Food Establishment began to earn money and fight with each other and review each other's books and say nasty things about each other's recipes and feel rotten about each other's good fortune, just about that time, there came curry. Some think it was beef Stroganoff, but in fact, beef Stroganoff had nothing to do with it. It began with curry. Curry with fifteen little condiments and Major Grey's mango chutney. The year of the curry is an elusive one to pinpoint, but this much is clear: it was before the year of quiche Lorraine, the year of paella, the year of vitello tonnato, the year of boeuf Bourguignon, the year of blanquette de veau, and the year of beef Wellington. It was before Michael stopped playing the piano, before Julia opened L'École des Trois Gourmandes, and before Craig had left his job as a bartender in Nyack, New York. It was the beginning, and in the beginning there was James Beard and there was curry and that was about all.

Historical explanations of the rise of the Food Establishment do not usually begin with curry. They begin with the standard background on the gourmet explosion—background that includes the traveling fighting men of World

War Two, the postwar travel boom, and the shortage of do-
mestic help, all of which are said to have combined to drive
the housewives of America into the kitchen.

This background is well and good, but it leaves out the
curry development. In the 1950s, suddenly, no one knew
quite why or how, everyone began to serve curry. Dinner
parties in fashionable homes featured curried lobster.
Dinner parties in middle-income homes featured curried
chicken. Dinner parties in frozen-food compartments featured curried rice. And with the arrival of curry, the first
fashionable international food, food acquired a chic, a gloss
of snobbery it had hitherto possessed only in certain upper-
income groups. Hostesses were expected to know that iceberg lettuce was *déclassé* and tunafish casseroles *de trop*.
Lancers sparkling rosé and Manischewitz were replaced on
the table by Bordeaux. Overnight rumaki had a fling and became a cliché.

The American hostess, content serving frozen spinach
for her family, learned to make a spinach soufflé for her
guests. Publication of cookbooks tripled, quadrupled, quin-
tupled; the first cookbook-of-the-month club, the Cookbook
Guild, flourished. At the same time, American industry realized that certain members of the food world—like James
Beard, whose name began to have a certain celebrity—could
help make foods popular. The French's mustard people
turned to Beard. The can-opener people turned to Poppy
Cannon. Pan American Airways turned to Myra Waldo. The
Potato Council turned to Helen McCully. The Northwest
Pear Association and the Poultry and Egg Board and the
Bourbon Institute besieged food editors for more recipes
containing their products. Cookbook authors were retained,
at sizable fees, to think of new ways to cook with bananas.

Or scallions. Or peanut butter. "You know," one of them would say, looking up from a dinner made during the peanut-butter period, "it would never have occurred to me to put peanut butter on lamb, but actually, it's rather nice."

Before long, American men and women were cooking along with Julia Child, subscribing to the Shallot-of-the-Month Club, and learning to mince garlic instead of pushing it through a press. Cheeses, herbs, and spices that had formerly been available only in Bloomingdale's delicacy department cropped up around New York, and then around the country. Food became, for dinner-party conversations in the sixties, what abstract expressionism had been in the fifties. And liberated men and women who used to brag that sex was their greatest pleasure began to suspect that food might be pulling ahead in the ultimate taste test.

Generally speaking, the Food Establishment—which is not to be confused with the Restaurant Establishment, the Chef Establishment, the Food-Industry Establishment, the Gourmet Establishment, or the Wine Establishment—consists of those people who write about food or restaurants on a regular basis, either in books, magazines, or certain newspapers, and thus have the power to start trends and, in some cases, begin and end careers. Most of them earn additional money through lecture tours, cooking schools, and consultancies for restaurants and industry. A few appear on radio and television.

The typical member of the Food Establishment lives in Greenwich Village, buys his vegetables at Balducci's, his bread at the Zito bakery, and his cheese at Bloomingdale's. He dines at the Coach House. He is given to telling you, apropos of nothing, how many soufflés he has been known to make in a short period of time. He is driven mad by a refrain he hears several times a week: "I'd love to have you for dinner," it goes, "but I'd be afraid to cook for you." He insists that there is no such thing as an original recipe; the important thing, he says, is point of view. He lists as one of his favorite cookbooks the original *Joy of Cooking* by Irma Rombauer, and adds that he wouldn't be caught dead using the revised edition currently on the market. His cookbook library runs to several hundred volumes. He gossips a good deal about his colleagues, about what they are cooking, writing, and eating, and whom they are talking to; about everything, in fact, except the one thing everyone else in the universe gossips about—who is sleeping with whom. In any case, he claims that he really does not spend much time with other members of the Food Establishment, though he does bump into them occasionally at Sunday lunch at Jim Beard's or at one of the publishing parties he is obligated to attend. His publisher, if he is lucky, is Alfred A. Knopf.

He takes himself and food very very seriously. He has been known to debate for hours such subjects as whether nectarines are peaches or plums, and whether the vegetables that Michael Field, Julia Child, and James Beard had one night at La Caravelle and said were canned were in fact canned. He roundly condemns anyone who writes more than one cookbook a year. He squarely condemns anyone who writes a cookbook containing untested recipes. Colleagues who break the rules and succeed are hailed almost as if they had happened on a new galaxy. "Paula Peck," he will say, in hushed tones of awe, "broke the rules in puff paste." If the Food Establishmentarian makes a breakthrough in cooking methods—no matter how minor and superfluous it may seem—he will celebrate. "I have just made a completely and utterly revolutionary discovery," said Poppy Cannon triumphantly one day. "I have just developed a new way of cooking asparagus."

There are two wings to the Food Establishment, each in mortal combat with the other. On the one side are the revolutionaries—as they like to think of themselves—the home economists and writers and magazine editors who are industry-minded and primarily concerned with the needs of the average housewife. Their virtues are performance, availability of product, and less work for mother; their concern is with improving American food. "There is an awe about Frenchiness in food which is terribly precious and has kept American food from being as good as it could be," says Poppy Cannon, the leader of the revolutionaries. "People think French cooking is gooking it up. All this kowtowing to so-called French food has really been a hindrance rather than a help." The revolutionaries pride themselves on discovering short cuts and developing convenience foods; they justify the compromises they make and the loss of taste that results by insisting that their recipes, while unquestionably not as good as the originals, are probably a good deal better than what the American housewife would prepare if left to her own devices. When revolutionaries get together, they talk about the technical aspects of food: how to ripen a tomato, for example; and whether the extra volume provided by beating eggs with a wire whisk justifies not using the more convenient electric beater.

On the other side are the purists or traditionalists, who see themselves as the last holdouts for haute cuisine. Their virtue is taste; their concern primarily French food. They are almost missionary-like, championing the cause of great food against the rising tide of the TV dinner, clamoring for better palates as they watch the children of America raised on a steady diet of Spaghetti Os. Their contempt for the revolutionaries is eloquent: "These people, these home economists," said Michael Field distastefully, "—they skim the iridescent froth off the gourmet department, and it comes out tasting like hell." When purists meet, they discuss each other; very occasionally, they talk about food: whether one ought to put orange peel into boeuf Bourguignon, for example, and why lamb tastes better rare.

Although the purists do not reach the massive market available to the revolutionaries, they are virtually celebrities. Their names conjure up a sense of style and taste; their appearance at a benefit can mean thousands of dollars for hospitals, charities, and politicians. The Big Four of the Food Establishment are all purists—James Beard, Julia Child, Michael Field, and Craig Claiborne.

Claiborne, a Mississippi-born man who speaks softly, wears half-glasses, and has a cherubic reddish face that resembles a Georgia peach, is probably the most powerful man in the Food Establishment. From his position as food editor of the *New York Times*, he has been able to bring down at least one restaurant (Claude Philippe's Pavillon), crowd customers into others, and play a critical part in developing new food tastes. He has singlehandedly revived sorrel and cilantro, and, if he could have his way, he would singlehandedly stamp out iceberg lettuce and garlic powder. To his dismay, he played a large part in bringing about the year of beef Wellington. "I hate the stuff," he says.

In his thirties, after too many unhappy years in public relations and the armed forces, Claiborne entered the Lausanne Hotel School to study cooking. On his return—and after a brief fling bartending—he began to write for *Gourmet* magazine and work for Ann Seranne's public-relations firm, handling such products as the Waring Blender and Fluffo the Golden Shortening. In 1957 he was hired by the *Times*, and he unabashedly admits that his job has been a dream come true. He loves it, almost as much as he loves eating, though not nearly as much as he loves cooking.

Claiborne is happiest in his Techbuilt house in Springs, East Hampton, which overlooks an herb garden, an over-sized swimming pool, and Gardiner's Bay. There, he, his next-door neighbor Pierre Franey—whom he calls "my arm and my dear friend"—and a number of other chefs go fish-ing, swap recipes, and whip up meals for fifty guests at a time. The menus are logged into a small leatherbound note-book in which Claiborne records every meal he eats throughout the year. During the winter, Claiborne lives in Greenwich Village. His breakfasts often consist of Sara Lee frozen croissants. His other daily meals are taken in restau-rants, and he discusses them as if he were serving penance. "That," he says firmly, "is the thing I like least about my job."

Six years ago Claiborne began visiting New York restau-rants incognito and reviewing them on a star system in the Friday *Times*; since that time, he has become the most en-vied, admired, and cursed man in the food world. Restaurant owners decry his Francophilia and can barely control their tempers while discussing his prejudice against large-management corporations and in favor of tiny, ethnic restau-rants. His nit-picking constantly irritates. Among some of the more famous nits: his censure of a Pavillon waiter who allowed his pencil to peek out; his disapproval of the salt and pepper shakers at L'Étoile, and this remark about Lutèce: "One could wish that the owner, Monsieur Surmain, would dress in a more reserved and elegant style to better match his surroundings."

Surmain, a debonair man who wears stylish striped shirts, sputters when Claiborne's name is mentioned. "He said in a restaurant of this sort I should wear a tuxedo," said Surmain. "What a bitchy thing. He wants me to act like a headwaiter."

The slings and arrows of outrage fly at Claiborne—and not only from restaurateurs. Carping about Craig is practically a parlor game in the food world. Everything he writes is pored over for its true significance. It is suggested, for example, that the reason Craig criticized proprietor Stuart Levin's clothes in his recent review of Le Pavillon had to do with the fact that Levin fawned over him during his two visits to the restaurant. It is suggested that the reason Craig praised the clothes of Charles Masson of Grenouille in the same review had to do with the fact that Masson ignores Craig entirely too much. It is suggested that Craig is not a nice person; and a story is offered to support the thesis, all about the time he reviewed a new restaurant owned by a friend after the friend begged him to wait a few weeks. His criticisms, it is said, drove the friend to drink.

But the fact of the matter is that Craig Claiborne does what he does better than anyone else. He is a delight to read. And the very things that make him superb as a food critic— his integrity and his utter incorruptibility—are what make his colleagues loathe him.

"Everyone thinks about Craig too much," says cookbook author and consultant Mimi Sheraton. "The truth is that he is his own man and there is no way to be a friend of his. He is the only writer who is really honest. Whether or not he's reliable, whether or not you like him, he is honest. I know *Cue* isn't—I used to write for them. *Gourmet* isn't. And Michael Field is just writing for Craig Claiborne."

Whenever members of the Food Establishment tire of discussing Craig they move on to discuss Craig's feuds—though in all fairness, it must be said that Claiborne is usually the less active party to the feuds. The feud currently absorbing the Food Establishment is between Claiborne and Michael Field. Field, who burst into stardom in the Food Establishment after a career as half of the piano team of Appleton & Field, is an energetic, amusing, frenetic man whose recent rise and subsequent candor have won him few friends in the food world. Those who are not his admirers have taken to passing around the shocking tidbit—untrue—that Field had not been to Europe until 1967, when he visited Julia Child in Provence.

"Essentially," says Field, "the whole Food Establishment is a mindless one, inarticulate and not very cultivated. These idiots who attack me are furious because they think I just fell into it. Well, let me tell you, I used to make forty soufflés in one day and throw them out, just to find the right recipe."

Shortly after his first cookbook was published, Field began reviewing cookbooks for the *New York Review of Books*, a plum assignment. One of his first articles, an attack on *The Fannie Farmer Cookbook* which centered on its fondue recipe, set off a fracas that produced a furious series of argumentative letters, in themselves a hilarious inadvertent parody of letters to highbrow magazines. Recently, he reviewed *The Thousand Recipe Chinese Cookbook*—a volume that was voted winner of the R. T. French (mustard) Tastemaker Award (chosen by one hundred newspaper food editors and roughly analogous in meaning to landing on the Best Dressed List). In his attack on Gloria Bley Miller's book, he wrote: "It would be interesting to know why, for example, Mrs. Miller's recipe for hot mustard requires the cook to bring one cup of water to a boil and then allow it to cool before adding one half cup of dry mustard? Surely Mrs. Miller must be aware that drinking and cooking water in China was boiled because it was often contaminated. . . ."

Mrs. Miller wrote in reply: "I can only suggest to Mr. Field . . . that he immerse his typewriter immediately in boiling water. There are many types of virulence in the world, and 'boiling the water first' is one of the best ways to disinfect anything."

The feud between Field and Claiborne had been simmering for several years, but Claiborne's review of the Time-Life cookbook turned it up to full boil. "He has a perfect right to dislike the book," said Field. "But his attack went far beyond that, into personalities." A few months after the review was published, Field counterpunched, with an article in *McCall's* entitled "New York's Ten Most Overrated Restaurants." It is in almost total opposition to Claiborne's *Guide to New York Restaurants;* in fact, reading Field's piece without having Claiborne's book alongside is a little like reading *Finnegans Wake* without the key.

For his part, Claiborne would just as soon not discuss Field—"Don't get me started," he said. And his attitude toward the Time-Life series has mellowed somewhat: he has finally consented to write the text of the *Time-Life Cookbook of Haute Cuisine* along with Franey. But some time ago, when asked, he was only too glad to defend his review. "Helen McCully (food editor of *House Beautiful*) said to me, 'How could you be so mean to Michael?' " he recalled. "I don't give a good God damn about Michael." His face turned deep red, his fists clenched, he stood to pace the room. "The misinformation! The inaccuracies in that book! I made a stack of notes thicker than the book itself on the errors in it. It's shameful."

Claiborne was so furious about the book, in fact, that he managed to intensify what was, until then, a one-sided feud between James Beard and himself. Beard, a genial, large, round man who receives guests in his Tenth Street house while seated, Buddha-like, on a large pouf, had been carrying on a mild tiff with Claiborne for some time. Just before the first Time-Life cookbook was published, the two men appeared together on the David Susskind Show, and in the course of the program, Beard held up the book and plugged it on the air. Afterward, Claiborne wrote a letter to Susskind, with carbon copy to Beard, saying that if he had known he was going to appear on the same show with the Time-Life cookbook, he never would have consented to go on.

(That Julia Child has managed thus far to remain above the internecine struggles of the food world probably has more to do with the fact that she lives in Cambridge, Massachusetts, well away from it all, than with her charming personality.)

The success of the Time-Life cookbook series is guaranteed, Claiborne's review notwithstanding. Offered by mail order to subscribers who care not one whit whether the soufflé on the cover is actually a meringue, the series rapidly signed up five hundred thousand takers—for all eighteen books! (The *New York Times* Cookbook, itself a blockbuster, has sold only two hundred thousand copies.) "The books, whatever their limits, are of enormous quality," says Field. "Every recipe works and is honestly conceived." Yet a number of those intimately connected with the books have complained about the limits Field parenthetically refers to, and most particularly about the technique of group journalism that has produced the books: apparently, the text, recipes, and photographs of some of the cookbooks have been done independently of each other.

"It's a joke," said Nika Hazelton, who is writing the text for the *Time-Life German Cookbook*. "First there is the writer—me, in this case, but I have nothing to do with the recipes or illustrations. Then there is the photographic staff, which takes recipes from old cookbooks, changes them a little, and photographs them. Then there is the kitchen, under Michael Field's supervision. I think Michael knows about French and Italian food, but he doesn't know quite as much about other cookery. The cook is John Clancy, a former cook in a short-order house who once worked for Jim Beard. I'm the only person connected with the project who knows languages besides French. There is a consultant who hasn't been in Germany for thirty years. My researcher's background is spending three years with the Morgan Bank. It's hilarious. I'm doing it only for the money."

The money that is available to members of the Food Establishment is not quite as much as they would have you think, but it is definitely enough to keep every last one of them in truffles. James Beard—who commands the highest fees and, though a purist, has the most ties with industry—recently turned down a hundred-thousand-dollar offer to endorse Aunt Jemima mixes because he didn't believe in their products. Retainers offered lesser stars are considerably smaller, but there are many jobs, and they suffice. Nevertheless, the impression persists that there are not enough jobs to go around. And because everyone in the food world is free-lancing and concerned with putting as many eggs into his basket as possible, it happens that every time someone gets a job, the rest feel that they have lost one.

Which brings us to the case of Myra Waldo. An attractive, chic woman who lives on upper Fifth Avenue, Miss Waldo published her first cookbook in 1954, and since then she has been responsible for forty-two others. Forty-two cookbooks! In addition, she does four radio spots a day for WCBS, is roving editor of *Family Circle* magazine, is retained by Pan American Airways, and recently landed the late Clementine Paddleford's job as food editor of *This Week* magazine. Myra Waldo has never been a favorite in the Food Establishment: she is far too successful. Furthermore, although *she* once made forty-eight soufflés over a July Fourth weekend, she is not a truly serious cook. (To a visitor who wanted a recipe for a dinner party, she suggested duck in a sauce made of frozen orange juice, Melba sauce, red wine, cognac, lemon juice, and a can of Franco-American beef gravy.) For years it has been rumored that Miss Waldo produces as many cookbooks as she does because she clips recipes and pastes them right onto her manuscript pages, or because she has a gigantic staff—charges she denies. But when she landed the *This Week* job, one that nearly everyone else in the Food Establishment had applied for, the gang decided that too much was too much. Shortly afterward, she went to the Cookbook Guild party, and no one except James Beard even said hello to her.

Said Beard: "You could barely move around at that party for fear someone would bite you in the back."

How much longer life in the Food Establishment—with its back-biting, lip-smacking, and pocket-jingling—will go on is hard to tell. There are some who believe the gourmet explosion that began it all is here to stay and that fine cooking is on the increase. "Of course it will last," said Poppy Cannon, "just in the way sculpture will last. We need it. It is a basic art. We ought to have a National Academy of the Arts to represent the art of cooking."

Others are less sure. They claim that the food of the future will be quite different: precooked, reconstituted, and frozen dishes with portion control. "The old cuisine is gone for good and dying out," says Mrs. Hazelton. "Ultimately, cooking will be like an indoor sport, just like making lace and handiwork."

Whatever happens, the Food Establishment at this moment has the power to change the way America eats. And in fact, about all it is doing is showing how to make a better piecrust and fill a bigger breadbox.

"What fascinates me," says Mimi Sheraton, "is that the more interest there is in gourmet food, the more terrible food is for sale in the markets. You can't buy an unwaxed cucumber in this country, the bread thing everyone knows about, we buy overtenderized meat and frozen chicken. You can't buy a really fresh egg because they've all been washed in hot water so the shells will be clean. And the influence of color photography on food! Oil is brushed on to make it glow. When we make a stew, the meat won't sit on top, so we have to prop it up with oatmeal. Some poor clod makes it at home and it's like buying a dress a model has posed in with the back pinned closed. As a result, food is marketed and grown for the purpose of appearances. We are really the last generation who even has a vague memory of what food is supposed to taste like.

"There have been three revolutionary changes in the food world in past years," Miss Sheraton continued. "The pressure groups have succeeded in changing the labeling of foods, they've succeeded in cutting down the amounts of pesticides used on foods, and they've changed the oversized packages used by the cereal and cracker people. To me, it's interesting that not one of these stories began with a food writer. Where are they, these food writers? They're off wondering about the boeuf en daube and whether the quiche was authentic."

Yes, that's exactly where they are. "Isn't it all a little too precious?" asks Restaurant Associates president Joseph Baum. "It's so elegant and recherché, it's like overbreeding a collie." But, after all, someone has to worry about the boeuf en daube and whether the quiche was authentic—right? And there is so much more to do. So many soufflés to test and throw out. So many ways of cooking asparagus to discover. So many patés to concoct. And so many things to talk about. Myra's new book. The record Poppy is making. Why Craig finally signed on to Time-Life Cookbooks. Michael's latest article. So much more to do. So many things to talk about. . . .

"If You're a Little Mouseburger, Come With Me. I Was a Mouseburger And I Will Help You."

I don't know anyone who has had professional contact with Helen Gurley Brown who is not fascinated by her. You probably don't believe that, but it's true. In the three years I wrote for Cosmopolitan, *she managed to drive me absolutely crazy with her passion for italics, exclamation points, upbeat endings, and baby simpleness. She once insisted on translating all the common French phrases I had used in an article—and translated almost every one of them wrong. But still, there is something about her. . . .*

February 1970

They are still screaming at her after all these years. They are still saying that Helen Gurley Brown is some kind of scarlet woman, for God's sakes, leading the young women of America into reckless affairs, possibly with married men. And every time they say it she sits there, little puckers beginning in her chin, and waits for the moment when the talk show will be over and she can run offstage and burst into tears. You might think that by now they would stop screaming—after all, this small, thin, dreadfully sincere woman is not to blame for the moral turpitude in America; you might think that by now Helen Gurley Brown would stop crying—after all, her attackers simply do not, cannot understand. But no. Just the other night, it happened again. On the Merv Griffin Show or the Joey Bishop Show. One or the other. She was just sitting there, talking in her underslung voice about how a single girl must go to lunch with married men, that a single girl with no other men in her life must somehow make the men who are there serve a purpose. She finished her little spiel and the screaming began. A singer on the panel started it. "Is this the kind of thing we want the young women of our country to listen to?" he said. "I wouldn't want any daughter of mine to go and date a married man." Then he turned to the audience and said, "Everyone out there who agrees with me, raise your hand or clap." And it began. Thunderous applause. Hundreds of hands flapping on the monitors. And as soon as the show was over, Helen Gurley Brown began to cry.

As it happens, Helen Gurley Brown cries quite a lot. She cried for three hours at Trader Vic's the night Jerry Lewis attacked her on the Tonight Show. She cried one day in the beauty parlor just after returning from a trip to see her mother. She cried the day a Hearst executive refused to let her run a cover of *Cosmopolitan* magazine because there was too much boosom showing. (That's the way she pronounces it. *Boo*som.) She cried the day Richard E. Berlin, President of the Hearst Corporation, put his foot down over a cover line that said, "The Pill That Makes Women More Responsive to Men." She cries all the time because people don't understand her. Jerry Lewis does not understand her, her mother does not understand her, and from time to time, the Hearst Corporation does not understand her. They don't understand what she is trying to do. They don't understand that she knows something they don't know. She knows about the secretaries, the nurses, the telephone-company clerks who live out there somewhere, miles from psychiatrists, plastic surgeons, and birth-control clinics. Only eight per cent of *Cosmopolitan*'s readers are in New York City—the rest are stuck in the wilds, coping with their first pair of false eyelashes and their first fling with vaginal foam and their first sit-down dinners and their first orgasms. These are the girls who read Helen Gurley Brown's *Single Girl's Cookbook* and learn—yes, *learn*—that before guests arrive for dinner it is smart to put out the garbage. These are the girls who buy *Cosmopolitan* and swallow whole such tidbits of advice as: "Rub your thighs together when you walk. The squish-squish sound of nylon...has a frenzying effect." These are the girls who have to be told How to Tell If He's a Married Man. You don't believe there are girls who cannot tell if a man is married? Listen, then, to this letter to Helen Gurley Brown from a young lady in Savannah, Georgia:

> My problem is a common one. I am an expectant un-wed mother.... The father of my child turned his back on me after he found out. Besides, he was married. However, I was not aware of this until after our affair

had begun, and too weak to break it off until I realized he had never been serious about me. By this time it was too late.

Helen Gurley Brown knows about these girls. She understands them. And don't you see? *She is only trying to help*.

We are sitting in her yellow-and-orange office across the street from Hearst headquarters at Fifty-seventh Street and Eighth Avenue in New York. On the floor is a large stuffed tiger. On the bulletin board is a picture of her husband, David. She calls him Lambchop. On the wall is a long magazine rack containing, along with a number of popular periodicals, the last twelve months of *Cosmopolitan* magazine. Read all about it. Why I Wear My False Eyelashes to Bed. I Was a Nude Model. I Was Raped. I Had a Hysterectomy. On her desk—along with some dental floss she uses before all editorial meetings—is a tearsheet of the next in a series of advertisements she writes for *Cosmopolitan;* this one, of a luscious girl, her hand poised deftly over her cleavage, has the following to say:

What does a girl do if she's wearing a hairpiece and she and her date are getting quite romantic? Well, we all know that a hairpiece can't live through very much in the way of stress and strain so I just take out the pins and take mine off. So far no boy I've known has ever fainted dead away because everything that basically *counts* is me . . . adding extra hair is just an *accessory*. When I think of all the subterfuge and pretending girls once had to go through I'm thankful I live now when you can be truthful . . . and there's a wonderful

magazine to help me be the honest female-female I
really am. I love that magazine. I guess you could say
I'm That COSMOPOLITAN Girl.

   Helen Gurley Brown is now in her fifth year as editor-in-
chief of *Cosmopolitan*. She took it over when she was forty-
three and it was in trouble, turned it around, breathed new
life and new image into it, became the only editor in
America to resurrect a dying magazine. She is now forty-
eight and tiny, with tiny wrists, tiny face, tiny voice. "I once
heard her lose her temper," a former *Cosmo* editor recalls,
"and it sounded like a little sparrow—she was chirping as
loud as she could but you still couldn't hear her." She wears
Rudi Gernreich dresses, David Webb jewelry, a Piaget
watch, expensive hairpieces, custom-cut false eyelashes—
but it never quite seems to come together properly. An ear-
ring keeps falling off. A wig is askew. A perfect matched
stocking has a run. All of which not-quite-right effect is in-
tensified because Helen Gurley Brown relentlessly talks
about her flat chest, her nose job, her split ends, her adolescent acne, her forty-minute regimen of isometrics and exer-
cises to stay in shape. She does not bring up these faults to
convince you she is unattractive but rather to show you
what can be done, what any girl can do if she really tries.
"Self-help," she says. "I wish there were better words, but that
is my whole credo. You cannot sit around like a cupcake asking other people to come and eat you up and discover your
great sweetness and charm. You've got to make yourself
more cupcakable all the time so that you're a better cupcake
to be gobbled up." That's the way she talks when she gets
carried away—exhortation, but in the style of girlish advertising copy. She talks about "hot-fudge-sundae-kind-of-

pleasure" and "good-old-fashioned-popcorn-eating-being-transported-to-another-world-going-to-the-movies."   Ten years as an advertising copywriter pays off for this girl. Yes sir. She can package anything. Titles for articles fall out of her mouth involuntarily. A staff member will suggest an article idea, and if she likes it, she has the title in an instant. The Oh-So-Private World of the Nurse, she will squeal. Or The Bittersweet World of the Hillbilly Girl. Or The Harried, Happy World of a Girl Buyer. One day someone suggested an article about how most girls worry about having orgasms. "Yes!" cried Mrs. Brown. "We'll call it 'It Never Really Happens to Me.' "

I am in Helen Gurley Brown's office because I am interviewing her, a euphemism for what in fact involves sitting on her couch and listening while she volunteers answers to a number of questions I would never ask. What she is like in bed, for example. Very good. Whether she enjoys sex. Very much. Always has. Why she did not marry until she was thirty-seven. Very neurotic. Wasn't ready. It all seems to pour out of her, her past, her secrets, her fears, her innermost hopes and dreams. Says her husband, David, "Whether it was group therapy or what, there's nothing left inside Helen. It all comes out."

It all comes out—in interviews, on television, in editorial conferences, in memoranda, in the pages of her magazine. Helen Gurley Brown spends twelve hours a day worrying, poring over, agonizing about her magazine; if her insomnia is acting up, she may spend most of the night. She writes end-less memos, in lower-case letters, to her writers, full of suggestions for articles she is particularly concerned about. "would like to go into a little detail about what goes through a girl's *head* as she is unable to have an orgasm," went one recent memo. "maybe a soliloquy. this subject has been treated so *clinically*...as though she couldn't do pushups...." She writes memos to her editors praising them, nudging them, telling them how to fix stories that need fixing. "She has a very clear picture of what will and will not fit her magazine," said Hearst editor-at-large Jeannette Wagner. "If she sends you back an article with a note that says, 'I want a lead that says thus-and-such,' you go back and do exactly what she says."

She works over every piece that goes into the magazine, doing the kind of line-by-line editing most editors leave to their juniors—rewriting, inserting exclamation points and italics and capitalized words and *Cosmopolitan* style into everything. "I want every article to be baby simple," she often says. Not surprisingly, most of the magazine sounds as if it were written by the same person. And, in a way, it is. *Cosmopolitan is* Helen Gurley Brown. Cute. Girlish. Exhortative. Almost but not quite tasteless. And in its own insidious, peculiar way, irresistible. Says *Cosmo* articles editor Roberta Ashley: "Helen manages to walk that line between vulgarity and taste, which isn't easy. The magazine is like a very sexy girl—you don't mind that her dress is cut down to her navel because her hair is clean. If her hair were dirty, you'd be revolted."

And if, at times, Helen Gurley Brown and her magazine are offensive, it is only because almost every popular success is offensive. Mrs. Brown—like Hugh Hefner and Dorothy Schiff, to name two other irritating publishing successes—offends because she is proving, at sizable financial profit, the old Mencken dictum that no one ever went broke underestimating the intelligence of the American public. She is demonstrating, rather forcefully, that there are well over a million American women who are willing to spend sixty cents to read *not* about politics, *not* about the female liberation movement, *not* about the war in Vietnam, but merely about how to get a man.

I have not been single for years, but I read *Cosmopolitan* every month. I see it lying on the newsstands and I'm suckered in. How to Increase the Size of Your Bust, the cover line says. Or Thirteen New Ways to Feminine Satisfaction. I buy it, greedily, hide it deep within my afternoon newspaper, and hop on the bus, looking forward to—at the very least—a bigger bra size and a completely new kind of orgasm. Yes, I should know better. After all, I used to write for *Cosmopolitan* and make this stuff up myself. But she gets me every time. I get home—or sometimes, if I simply can't wait, I open it on the bus, being careful to remove my glove so that onlookers will see my wedding band and will know I'm not reading *Cosmopolitan* because I'm That COSMOPOLITAN Girl. And there it is. Buy a padded bra, the article on bustlines tells me. Fake it, the article on orgasm says. And I should be furious. But I'm not. Not at all. How can you be angry at someone who's got your number?

In a recent article in the *Antioch Review* linking *Cosmopolitan* and *Playboy*, Peter Michelson wrote, "*Cosmopolitan*, or more likely the Hearst hierarchy, recognized how *Playboy* was making the world safe for pornography, and it very neatly cut itself in on the sex-profit nexus." That explanation, while interesting, gives the Hearst Corporation more credit than it is due. In 1964 about all the Hearst people realized was that *Cosmopolitan* was in bad shape. Circulation had dropped to under eight hundred thousand copies a month, below the advertising guarantee. Advertising was down to twenty-one pages an issue. Early in 1965 Helen Gurley Brown came to see Richard Deems, president of the Hearst Magazine Division, with a dummy for a new magazine. He had vaguely heard of her, had no idea she was at all controversial, and had never read her 1962 best seller, *Sex and the Single Girl*. But he liked her, he liked her idea for a magazine aimed at single women, and most of all, he liked her long list of companies that might be willing to advertise in such a magazine. It is safe to say that if Deems had thought that Helen Gurley Brown was going to turn *Cosmopolitan* into something that would repeatedly be called the female counterpart to *Playboy*, he would not have employed her. "We happen to be a company with a conscience about what it publishes," he said. "Our paperback division is the only book company that doesn't have a married-sex book. We're very studious about this kind of thing."

There are, of course, many similarities between *Cosmopolitan* and *Playboy*. Both magazines contain nudity. Both are concerned with sexual freedom of a sort. Both are headed by people who are the products of repressed, WASP backgrounds. Both publish the worst work of good writers. Both exalt material possessions. Both are somewhat deprecating to the opposite sex: *Playboy* turns its women into sexual objects; *Cosmopolitan* makes its men mindless creatures who can be toppled into matrimony by perfect soufflés, perfect martinis, and other sorts of perfectible manipulative techniques.

Recently Helen Gurley Brown even commissioned a *Playboy*-type foldout picture—of actor James Coburn, nude, his vital parts somewhat obscured by a potted palm. "It was a very pretty picture," said Mrs. Brown. "But ... I don't like to be in the position of turning James Coburn down ... but the particular picture I needed didn't come out of this shooting. The pictures were very hippie and mystical, strange and ethereal and a little sad, and Jesus, that isn't what I had in mind at all. I wanted a cute, funny, wonderful foxy picture, with that great mouth and marvelous teeth. I *am* going to do a foldout—I'll take another whack at it—but I haven't got the picture I want yet."

There is one major difference between *Playboy* and *Cosmopolitan*. The *Playboy* man has no problems. The *Cosmopolitan* girl has thousands. She has menstrual cramps, pimples, budget squeeze, hateful roommates. She cannot meet a man. She cannot think of what to say when she meets one. She doesn't know how to take off her clothes to get into bed with him. She doesn't know how to find a psychiatrist. She even gets raped, though only by rapists with somewhat unlikely dialogue. (In "I Was Raped," *Cosmopolitan* introduced the only rapist in history who lay down on his victim and murmured, "Let's make love.")

"It drives my management wild to be compared with *Playboy*," said Mrs. Brown. "We are not like *Playboy*. We are all the things we've been talking about—onward, upward, be it, do it, get out of your morass, meet some new men, don't accept, don't be a slob, be everything you're capable of. If you're a little mouseburger, come with me. I was a mouseburger and I will help you. You're so much more wonderful than you think. *Cosmopolitan* is shot full of this stuff although outsiders don't realize it. It is, in its way, an inspiration magazine."

There is very little that has happened to Helen Gurley Brown that she has not managed to extricate a rule from. Or

learn a lesson from. Or make a maxim of. Or see, in hind-
sight, that it was all part of a plan. If it weren't for her unhappy childhood, she says, she wouldn't be enjoying herself
so much now. If it weren't for her years of difficulty, she
would never have had such a drive to improve her lot. She
has led a hard life, a perfect life out of which to build inspirational books and an inspirational magazine.

She was born in Green Forest, Arkansas, in the Ozarks,
the second daughter of Cleo and Ira Gurley. Both her parents were schoolteachers, but her father turned to politics
and was elected to the state legislature. In 1925 he moved
his family to Little Rock. He was killed in a freak elevator
accident in the State Capitol Building seven years later. His
daughter Helen was ten and his daughter Mary was fourteen.

"That really changed our lives considerably," Helen Gurley
Brown remembered one day recently. "That sort of finished
things, finished a phase of my life which I never will get back.
The security. . . . They say a great deal of your life is formed by
the time you're about seven, so these drives and rages and am-
bitions and yearnings and needings and cravings of mine must
have been formed before that time, some of them. I never
have gotten to the bottom of all that. Why am I so driven? It
seems logically to have derived from things that happened to
me after my father died, but some of it must be residual from
very early. I don't know.

"But anyway, here we are in Little Rock, little fatherless
children. I don't think my mother and father were particularly happy together, but my father's death was a horren-
dous thing in her life. She and my father had been very poor.
She gets disgusted with me because I keep carrying on about

how poor I was. I always ate. I always looked O.K. I really never was eating pork and beans out of a can and putting cardboard in the soles of my shoes. But it's what you get in your head, it's how it seemed to you that motivates you. Whereas my parents were really poor, and just about the time things were beginning to go rather well, she and my father resolved whatever differences they had, poosh, he's taken away, snapped off.

"We stayed in Little Rock for about three years after my father's death," she continued. "But he left a limited amount of insurance and our house was mortgaged to the hilt. So because Mother felt we couldn't keep up the nice little standard of living in Little Rock on this particular stipend she had been left, she decided we'd all go move to Los Angeles. It was very brave and gutsy of her. But my sister didn't want to go to California. I didn't either. And my mother didn't level with us, because you didn't in those days. She said, 'Oh, I think it would be nice to go to California, we have relatives there.' So we move to California and Mary gets polio." She paused. "She was nineteen. There was no March of Dimes and there was nobody to help. Shlurp, in one big thing, in one year, it took all the money we had. I really got good and scared out of my wits about that time." Another pause. "I just didn't know what was going to become of us. It was still the end of the Depression, jobs were very hard to get and my sister—she's never walked again. I don't know, we were sort of a pitiful little tribe." Her voice cracked and she began to cry. "My word," she said. "I never talk about this any more." She daubed at her eyes with a handkerchief. "Well, this is the way I was for years. It was the three of us sort of huddled together. My sister was in a wheelchair and

needed constant care. My mother couldn't go back to work
or do anything for a number of years." Tears continued to
roll down her face. "I was terrified," she said.

The Gurleys moved to the East Side of Los Angeles near
the Los Angeles Orthopaedic Hospital, and Helen enrolled
at John H. Francis Polytechnic High School. Her memories
of that period—aside from her sister's illness—have mainly
to do with having acne. "I was kind of a cute little girl, but
who could see past these pus pustules?" Like that. She became a student leader, graduated as valedictorian, and was
taken to the prom by the student-body president. "It was the
coup of the year," she recalled with some amusement. "He
had a real case on me, because he got close enough to find
out what I was like. I always have to get men close enough to
me to be interested in me. I have to do what I call Sinking In
before they pay attention. I'm never anybody that some
man sees at a party and says, 'Get me her.' Never. But once
they get near me and I turn on what I call Plain Girl Power—
well, it worked with the student-body president."

Following high school and a year at Woodbury Business
College, Helen went to work answering fan mail at radio station KHJ to pay for her second year at college. Her mother
worked in the marking room at Sears Roebuck. Her sister
did telephone work for the Hooper rating service. Then Mrs.
Gurley and Mary moved back to Arkansas and Helen was
left as a single girl in Los Angeles. Friends who knew her in
the 1940s, when she held eighteen consecutive secretarial
jobs, remember her as a shy, self-effacing, attractive girl who
always did the sorts of clever things that seemed astonishing
twenty years ago, like putting egg in spinach salad. She was,
they recall, completely neurotic about money. She sent one
week's salary each month to her family and she was con-

vinced no one would ever marry her because of her financial obligations.

To make ends meet, she took the bus to work, drove her car only on weekends with gas she pumped at the serve-yourself station on Beverly Boulevard, brought her lunch to the office in a paper sack, read other people's newspapers, made her own clothes, traveled by Greyhound bus. She tried every angle. Because she washed her hair in Woolite, she wrote the president of the company to tell him—and he sent her a free box of the stuff. She wrote an unsolicited memo to the proprietor of the beauty salon in her office lobby telling him how to hype up business—and he did her hair for nothing. She entered the *Glamour* magazine Ten Girls with Taste Contest three years in a row, and finally won. "I used to enter all the contests," she said. "I bought so many bars of Lux soap to enter the 'I like Lux soap be-cause...' contest. I couldn't enter under my own name be-cause I worked in an advertising agency, so I would send them to Mary and say, 'Please, Mary, have a picture made of yourself in a wheelchair and send these off.' Well, that didn't work. That's one that failed. But I did it. I tried."

She tried everything. Vitamin therapy. Group therapy. Psychoanalysis. Hair therapy. Skin therapy. Her persistent self-improvement dazzled her friends. "She decided the kind of person she wanted to be, the milieu in which she wanted to live, how she wanted to look," said one longtime California associate. "In a very real sense, she invented her-self." There were a number of men in Helen Gurley's life—two agents, a married advertising executive, and a Don Juan whom she spent nine years off and on with—but to hear her tell it, her job always came first. She became secretary to Don Belding, a partner in Foote, Cone & Belding, and after five years she was made a copy writer. "It was so heady," she recalled in a near whisper. "I adored it. Instead of making a hundred dollars a week I'm making ten thousand dollars a year, and this is in 1955 and that was considerable money for a girl then, very heady. You know, everything adds up. It's what I keep saying in my books and in *Cosmo*. If you do every little thing you can do in your own modest position, one thing leads to another. So *do* it and *be* it and *write* the letters and *make* the phone calls and get *on* with it. And this is what I was doing every hour of the day, every day of the year.

"But I'm still living in my frugal way. I'm still bringing my lunch to the office. And I was conservative enough to have saved a little money. I had managed to save eight thousand dollars." One day Helen Gurley walked into a Beverly Hills used-car lot and paid five thousand dollars for a Mercedes-Benz. Cash. "The next weekend I went to the Beldings' ranch in total shock because of this money I spent. It just was not like me. I was in pain, physical pain. Everyone told me all the reasons I should have that car—that I was a successful writer and a gifted girl—they pumped me up and held my hand. But every time they looked at me I was sitting over in the corner in a catatonic heap thinking of the money.

"A week or so later a friend of mine set up this famous date with David Brown, whom she'd been saving for me. I thought it was going to be a big thing. I felt it in my bones before I met him. She'd been talking about him for three years, and it felt right. It was an interesting, lovely evening. And he took me to my car after dinner. I could see him looking at this car, this nice car. And I said, 'Yes, I just bought it and I paid all cash for it.' And that was a nice thing, he liked the fact that I'd been able to save all that money, because he had been married to very extravagant women, particularly his last wife."

Helen Gurley and David Brown were married one year later, in September 1959, at the Beverly Hills City Hall. He is now vice-president and chief of story operations at 20th Century-Fox, and his wife continually says she could never have become what she has become without him. He gave her the idea of writing *Sex and the Single Girl*. He gave her the idea of aiming a magazine at single women. He was once an editor of *Cosmopolitan;* and in her early days there, he helped her run the magazine, rushing over in taxicabs for street-corner conferences about copy. He still writes all the cover blurbs for the magazine. Both Browns live work-oriented lives—long office hours, dinners out with business friends. They spend at least one night a week at Trader Vic's with Darryl Zanuck; they travel to Palm Springs and the Riviera with Richard Zanuck. Several nights a week they eat at home, in their Park Avenue apartment, and spend the evening working.

At one point last year, Mrs. Brown was also emceeing a television show and overseeing the editing of Hearst's *Eye* magazine. Both operations are now defunct, and she is left with just *Cosmopolitan*. Now selling 1,073,211 copies a month. Now pulling in 784 advertising pages a year—compared with 1964's 259. There are still the little setbacks, of course: old friends who are jealous; reader complaints over increasing nudity in the magazine; the Hearst Corporation's censorship. But though Helen Gurley Brown cries frequently, she cries much less now than she used to.

Why just the other day she managed to get through a major flap without crying once. It all had to do with the breast memorandum. Perhaps you remember it—one of her

staff members leaked it to *Women's Wear Daily*, and every
newspaper in the country picked it up. The memo began,
"We are doing an article on how men should treat women's
breasts in lovemaking. It will either help us sell another
100,000 copies or stop publication of *Cosmopolitan* altogether." Its purpose? "To help a lot of men make a lot of girls
more happy." It went on to say . . . But stop. Let her tell the
story.

"It started with my idea of how boosoms should be handled," she said. "Ninety-nine per cent of the articles here are
assigned by the other editors, but this particular thing was a
secret of mine that I felt only I understood. I called my own
writer in California and told her about it. She tried it and
turned it in and it was beautiful, but *God*, it didn't have *anything* to do with how men should treat women's boosoms. It
had to do with *love* and it had to do with *companionship* and
the wonderful relationship between men and women, but it
just didn't have *anything* to do technically with the subject.
I wanted techniques. What does she like and how does she
tell him and what does he do and how does he shape up. So
I called my writer and said, 'This is your personal reminis-
cence of all your love affairs, and fascinating as it is, it
doesn't have *anything* to do with boobs.' And she said, 'I
know. Can you supply me with any material?'

"That's when I sat down and wrote my memo to the girls
in the office. Just give me your thoughts about boosoms, I
said. Has anybody ever been a real idiot in making love to
you? How could men improve their techniques? What
would you like done that's not being done? I just got a wonderful response. All the girls responded except two. I'd like
to know who the two were because I don't think they'd be
happy at *Cosmopolitan*, but I had no way of knowing be-

cause a lot of girls didn't sign their memos. I've sent many memos before—give me your definition of a bitch, have you ever dated a very wealthy man—and this was just another one of those memos. Then I saw it in *Women's Wear Daily* and I really did hit the roof. A lot of people said, Ho, ho, ho, how lucky can you be? You probably mailed it yourself in an unmarked envelope. But that's not true, because I tread a very careful path with Hearst management and I don't want to get them exercised about anything. If I just very quietly develop these articles and show them the finished product, it's much better. But this big brouhaha started because this little bitch, whoever she was, sent the memo to *Women's Wear*, and I would still fire her if I knew who she was. Because then the turmoil started. My management said to me, We want to see a copy of the boosom article the minute it's finished. I didn't want this attention to be called to what I was doing. Furthermore, we have trouble with supermarkets in the South and I didn't want them stirred up ahead of time.

"Well, the girls wrote their wonderful memos, I put two other writers on the story—because the girl in California suddenly got very haughty and said she didn't want to deal with the material. She just went absolutely crackers about the whole thing. So these two writers took it on and between them they turned in wonderful stuff, their own ideas plus all my material. I got this fantastic article. But my management won't let me run it. The actual use of anatomical words bugs them. Well, you cannot talk about love and relationships when you're talking about how to handle a breast. You must be anatomical. You've got to say a few things about what to do. I'm not mad at them—they do it because they're afraid we'll have too much flack. But I plan to lie low

for a while and come back with my boosom article later. I
read it tenderly, like a little love letter, every so often. I'll try
it again after a while."

One day a couple of years ago, a *Cosmopolitan* editor named
Harriet LaBarre called me and asked if I wanted to write an
article on how to start a conversation. They would pay six
hundred dollars for one thousand words. Yes, I would. Fine,
she said, she would send me a memo Helen had written on
the subject. The memo arrived, a breezy little thing filled
with suggestions like "Remember what the great Cleveland
Amory says—shyness is really selfishness" and "Be sure to
debunk the idea that it is dangerous to approach strangers." I
read it and realized with some embarrassment that I had already written the article the memo wanted, in slightly different form—for *Cosmopolitan*, no less. I called Harriet
LaBarre and told her.

"Omigod," she said. "And I even edited it."

We talked it over and decided that I might as well take
the assignment anyway.

"After all," said Mrs. LaBarre, "if it doesn't bother us to
run the same article twice, it shouldn't bother you to *write* it
twice."

"I have just one question, though," I said. "What is this
about the great Cleveland Amory and his theory that shyness is just selfishness?"

"Did she say that?" said Mrs. LaBarre. "She must be kidding—I don't even think she likes Cleveland Amory."

A few weeks later I turned the article in, and Harriet
LaBarre called. "We're going to run it," she said, "but there
are two things we want to change."

"All right," I said.

"First of all, I was wrong about Cleveland Amory," she said. "I'm afraid we do have to say that shyness is really selfishness."

"But shyness *isn't* really selfishness," I said.

"Well, I know, but that's the way we have to put it."

"What's the second thing?" I said.

"Well, it's just one little change Helen made, but I wanted to read it to you. You have a sentence that reads, 'It is absurd to think that any girl who asks a nice-looking man how to get to Rockefeller Center will be bundled up in a burlap bag and sold into a Middle Eastern harem.' "

"Yes," I said, realizing it wasn't much of a sentence.

"Well, Helen changed it to read, 'The notion that any girl who asks a nice-looking man how to get to Rockefeller Center is immediately bundled up in a burlap bag and sold into a Middle Eastern harem is as antique and outmoded a myth as the notion that you can't take a bath while you're menstruating.' "

"What?"

"Is that all right?" she said.

"Is that all *right*? Of course it's not all right. How did that particular image get into my article?"

"I don't really know," said Harriet LaBarre. "We're thinking of doing a piece on menstruation and maybe it was on her mind."

I hung up, convinced I had seen straight to the soul of Helen Gurley Brown. Straight to the foolishness, the tastelessness her critics so often accused her of. But I was wrong. She really isn't that way at all. She's just worried that somewhere out there is a girl who hasn't taken a bath during her period since puberty. She's just worried that somewhere out there is a girl whose breasts aren't being treated properly. She's just worried that somewhere out there is a mouse-burger who doesn't realize she has the capability of becoming anything, anything at all, anything she wants to, of becoming Helen Gurley Brown, for God's sake. And don't you see? *She is only trying to help.*

The Fountainhead Revisited

Ayn Rand is not easy to write about—and not just because she doesn't cooperate. One example will suffice. When I was interviewing her editor Ed Kuhn he told me that she was furious because an article in Life *magazine had described her as wearing a tricornered hat and a cape. "She has never worn a tricornered hat and a cape," said Kuhn. "I don't know about the cape," I told him, "but Hiram Haydn, who used to be her editor, told me that whenever he met her for lunch she wore a tricornered hat." "Oh," said Kuhn. "Well, it must have been the cape that bothered her." I went home to my bookshelf, where Miss Rand's works were in temporary residence, pulled out a recent paperback of hers, and there on the cover was a picture of her wearing a cape. I decided not to*

bother Kuhn with the information. It would just
have confused him.

May 1968

Twenty-five years ago, Howard Roark laughed. Standing
naked at the edge of a cliff, his face gaunt, his hair the color
of bright orange rind, his body a composition of straight,
clean lines and angles, each curve breaking into smooth,
clean planes, Howard Roark laughed. It was probably a
soundless laugh; most of Ayn Rand's heroes laugh sound-
lessly, particularly while making love. It was probably a
laugh with head thrown back; most of Ayn Rand's heroes do
things with their heads thrown back, particularly while dealing with the rest of mankind. It was probably a laugh that
had a strange kind of simplicity; most of Ayn Rand's heroes
act with a strange kind of simplicity, particularly when what
they are doing is of a complex nature.

Whatever else it was, Howard Roark's laugh began a
book that has become one of the most astonishing phenom-
ena in publishing history. *The Fountainhead* by Ayn Rand
was published on May 8, 1943, by the Bobbs-Merrill
Company, at the then-staggering price of three dollars. Its
author, a Russian émigrée with a Dutch-boy haircut, had
written the 728-page book over a period of seven years, six
months of which were spent hanging around an architect's
office learning the lingo of the profession Howard Roark was
to exemplify so romantically. The book was turned down by
twelve publishers; the editor-in-chief of Bobbs finally
bought it over the objections of his publisher.

In the years since, *The Fountainhead* has sold over two and a half million copies in hard and soft cover. Bobbs-Merrill, which has just issued its thirty-second printing, a twenty-fifth anniversary deluxe edition which sells for eight dollars, calls it "the book that just won't stop selling." Along with Miss Rand's other blockbuster, *Atlas Shrugged*, it forms the theoretical basis for the Rand philosophy known as Objectivism. New American Library considers the two books the prize possessions of its paperback backlist. "Once or twice a year we reissue these books," said Edward Kuhn, former editor-in-chief of NAL, who recently became publisher of the World Publishing Company, another Times-Mirror subsidiary. "And I'm not talking about a printing of ten thousand. These books are reprinted in runs of fifty and one hundred thousand copies. What this means is that every year one hundred thousand new people read *The Fountainhead*—a new generation of readers every five years. Other than with Fitzgerald and Hemingway—and I couldn't even say Faulkner and Sinclair Lewis—this just doesn't happen."

The Fountainhead is the story of Howard Roark, modern architect, and his fight for integrity, individualism, and ego-fulfillment against the altruistic parasites who believe in Gothic architecture, and more important, against the near heroes who do not believe the fight can be won. It is also the story of Roark's thoroughly peculiar love affair with one Dominique Francon (whose body is also a clean composition of straight, clean lines and angles, notwithstanding the fact that conventional curves might have been better). Miss Francon is first attracted to Roark while he is working splitting rocks in a granite quarry on her property; she is raped by him on page 219 of the new deluxe edition and page 209 in the paperback. When she discovers, somewhat later, that he is the only architect whose work she admires, she sets out to protect him from disappointment by making certain no one ever gives him a job. She marries two men just to tick him off. "Dominique is myself in a bad mood," Miss Rand once said.

The book ends in a blaze of ego when Roark blows up a housing project he has designed after details of it have been altered; he is ultimately acquitted; and he marries Dominique. They live happily ever after, one supposes, in a steel-and-glass house.

When *The Fountainhead* was published, almost every critic who reviewed it missed the point—that the welfare of society must always be subordinate to individual self-interest. Rather than dealing with this theme of ego, most of the reviewers treated it as a Big Book, and (with the exception of the critic for the *New York Times Book Review*, who compared it to *The Magic Mountain*) treated it badly. The reviewer for the daily *New York Times* called it "a whale of a book about architecture" and thought it overwritten and melodramatic. Wrote the critic for *Architectural Forum:* "The architecture profession, may the Lord protect it, has at last been made a background for a novel. According to its publishers, *The Fountainhead* will do for architects what *Arrowsmith* did for doctors. Though we do not recall precisely what *Arrowsmith* did for doctors, it seems likely that *The Fountainhead* may do a lot less for the architects."

Like most of my contemporaries, I first read *The Fountainhead* when I was eighteen years old. I loved it. I too missed the point. I thought it was a book about a strong-willed architect—Frank Lloyd Wright, my friends told me—and his love life. It was the first book I had ever read on modern architecture, and I found it fascinating. I deliberately skipped over all the passages about egotism and altruism. And I spent the next year hoping I would meet a gaunt, orange-haired architect who would rape me. Or failing that, an architect who would rape me. Or failing that, an architect. I am certain that *The Fountainhead* did a great deal more for architects than *Architectural Forum* ever dreamed: there were thousands of fat, pudgy nonarchitects who could not get dates during college because of the influence *The Fountainhead* had on foolish girls like me.

In any case, about a year after I read the book I sat in on a freshman-orientation seminar which discussed the book (among other novels it was suspected incoming Wellesley girls had read) and was shocked to discover:

- That Howard Roark probably shouldn't have blown up that housing project.
- That altruism was not bad in moderation.
- That the book I had loved was virtually a polemic.
- That its author was opposed to the welfare state.

I also learned, though not in the seminar, that architects were, for the most part, nothing like Howard Roark.

I recently reread *The Fountainhead*, and while I still have a great affection for it and recommend it to anyone taking a plane trip, I am forced to conclude that it is better read when one is young enough to miss the point. Otherwise, one cannot help thinking it is a very silly book. (*Atlas Shrugged*, the saga of a group of Roark-like heroes who go on strike, move to a small Atlantis somewhere in Colorado, and allow the world to go to pot in their absence, is not a silly book. It is a ridiculous book. It is also quite obviously a book by an author whose previous work readers have missed the point of. It is impossible to miss the point of *Atlas Shrugged*. Nevertheless, it is a book that cannot be put down, and therefore probably should not be picked up in the first place.)

"*The Fountainhead* was only an overture to ATLAS SHRUGGED," Miss Rand has written, emphasizing the disparity between the two books by italicizing the one and capitalizing the other. The philosophy of Objectivism which assumes such pollinating proportions in the latter was only blossoming in the former—though, according to Miss Rand's official biography, it had begun to develop in Miss Rand shortly after her birth.

Ayn (rhymes with pine) Rand was born in 1905 to Jewish parents in Petrograd. "I know they call it Leningrad now," she said years later, "but I still call it Petrograd." She grew up loving the romantic fiction of Victor Hugo, hating Communist ideology, and denouncing God. In 1926, after a Chicago relative offered to sponsor her passage to the United States, Miss Rand joyfully left for New York. As she sailed into Manhattan, she once recalled, "There was one skyscraper that stood out ablaze like the finger of God, and it seemed to me the greatest symbol of free man. . . . I made a mental note that someday I would write a novel with the skyscraper as a theme." The tallest skyscraper at that time was the elaborately Gothic Woolworth building.

In the seventeen years that elapsed between her vow and its execution, Miss Rand, among other things, lived at the Studio Club in Hollywood, was an extra in the film *The King of Kings*, wrote motion-picture scenarios, stuffed envelopes, waited on tables, and married Frank O'Connor, a painter, who is not to be confused with the short-story writer. (His painting of a skyscraper under construction adorns the cover of the deluxe edition of *The Fountainhead*.) In 1934 she and her husband moved to New York; in 1936 her first novel, *We the Living*, was published, and her play, *The Night of January 16*, a melodrama, ran seven months on Broadway. And she set to work—in architect Ely Jacques Kahn's office—on her new book.

By late 1940 she had completed one-third of the manuscript, then entitled *Second-Hand Lives*, and been rejected by twelve publishers. When funds ran out, she went to work as a reader at Paramount Pictures; there she showed her book to the late Richard Mealand, Paramount story editor. Mealand, who loved it, showed it to Archibald Ogden, editor-in-chief of Bobbs; Ogden, who loved it, sent it to Indianapolis to Bobbs president D. L. Chambers; Chambers, who hated it, sent it back with orders not to buy it. "I do not care much for allegories myself," he wrote, "I presume you will not wish to proceed further with your negotiations." Ogden wrote back: "If this is not the book for you, then I am not the editor for you." To which Chambers wired: "Far be it from me to dampen such enthusiasm. Sign the contract." Miss Rand signed—and received a modest one-thousand-dollar advance.

The final manuscript—seventy-five thousand words shorter than Miss Rand had written it—continued to displease Chambers. He suggested that the book be cut in half. Without telling Ogden, he ordered the first printing cut from twenty-five thousand copies to twelve thousand and insisted it be printed from type: there was no point in making plates for a book that would clearly never sell out its first printing.

And, of course, it did. *The Fountainhead*—the title was changed at Ogden's suggestion—has become known in the trade as the classic cult book. The classic book that made its own way. "It was the greatest word-of-mouth book I've ever been connected with," said Bobbs-Merrill's trade-division sales manager, William Finneran. "Over the years, we spent about two hundred fifty thousand dollars in advertising it, and we might as well have plowed it back into profits for all the good it did for us." Six slow months after publication—and its purchase by Warner Brothers for a film that starred Gary Cooper and Patricia Neal—sales began to build; ultimately, the book appeared on the best-seller list twenty-six times through 1945. "I did not know that I was predicting my own future," Ayn Rand once wrote, "when I described the process of Roark's success: 'It was as if an underground stream flowed through the country and broke out in sudden springs that shot to the surface at random, in unpredictable places.' "

As it happened, the places were not all that unpredictable. According to Finneran, the book first began to sell in small cities. A bookstore owner in Detroit told his customers he was not interested in their business unless they bought the book. A Friend of the public library in Cleveland demanded that the library buy twenty-five copies of it. A lady in Minneapolis gave it to all her friends and later claimed credit for the book's sales. "It started out with people in their thirties emerging from the Depression," said Finneran, "and I think if you put them through a computer you'd find they were people who have read three books in their whole lives, other than books they had to read in business, and the other two were *Gone with the Wind* and *Anthony Adverse*."

By 1950 an unorganized cult of Rand enthusiasts—none of whom, by the way, had missed the point—was at loose in the land. Miss Rand was then living in a house built by Richard Neutra in the San Fernando Valley, where she had moved six years earlier to write the script of *The Fountainhead*. (The movie, released in 1949, was not financially successful, but Miss Rand loved it. Not a line of her script was altered. "She told me she would blow up the Warner Brothers lot if we changed one word of her beautiful dialogue," said producer Henry Blanke. "And we believed her. Even Jack Warner believed her. He gave her a cigar.") There, she received a letter from a UCLA psychology student named Nathaniel Branden asking about the philosophical implication of her novel. Branden became her disciple—and since his family name is Blumenthal, it is probably no coincidence that his adopted name contains his mentor's last name. When he, his future wife, Barbara, and the O'Connors moved to New York a year later, Branden became the organizer of a group of Rand devotees who met every Saturday night at Miss Rand's East Thirties apartment. They were known as the Class of 1943, after The Book's publication date, and Miss Rand referred to them as "the children."

In 1957, after *Atlas Shrugged* was published by Random House, Branden opened the Nathaniel Branden Institute and has since graduated twenty-five thousand students schooled in the principles of Objectivism: that individualism is preferable to collectivism, selfishness to altruism, and nineteenth-century capitalism to any other kind of economic system. Those beliefs, which run loose through *The Fountainhead* and run amuck through *Atlas Shrugged* are expounded by Miss Rand and Branden in *The Objectivist Newsletter*, which has sixty thousand subscribers. Objectivists occasionally smoke cigarettes with dollar signs on them. They quote Howard Roark. Like John Galt, the Roark of *Atlas Shrugged*, Branden is an unabashed capitalist and bills his organization as "profit-making." Miss Rand is said to wear a gold dollar-sign brooch.

One would have liked to ask Miss Rand about that brooch, but she does not give interviews to nonsympathizers. One would have liked to ask her a number of other questions: how she feels about *The Fountainhead*'s continuing success, how she reacts when she thinks of the people in publishing who said it would never sell, what she does when she opens her royalty checks. Presumably, Ayn Rand laughs.

Makeover:

The Short, Unglamorous Saga
of a New, Glamorous Me

I spent about five years throwing desperate hints at magazine beauty editors about my passionate desire to be made over. When it finally happened it was one of the most depressing experiences of—well, if not of my life, then certainly of that month of my life. Like most of my friends who have been overexposed to fashion magazines, I had come to believe that cosmetic and plastic surgery could accomplish anything. Perhaps plastic surgery can—but I am here today, with my long face and drooping eyelid, to tell you that cosmetic surgery can do close to nothing.

This piece as it originally appeared in Cosmopolitan was edited in order to give it a peppy, upbeat ending—a Helen Gurley Brown special. I have restored the original, bleak, dismal, downbeat, depressing one.

BEFORE

May 1968

Monday

Cosmopolitan magazine is going to make me over. On Thursday. Don't know what they're going to make me over into, but plan to suggest they try for Faye Dunaway. Called husband to tell him news. "That's great, honey," he said. "That's fantastic. Terrific. Really marvelous." Husband over-reacting. Lupe doing my hair. Who, you may ask, is Lupe. Lupe spent summer doing Beautiful People's hair in Southampton, and when summer ended Beautiful People said, "Lupe, Lupe, we cannot get through the winter without you. You must come to New York." So he did. "He does all of high society," said Beauty Editor. "Good," said I, "because then he is used to coping with only moderately attractive people." Mark Traynor doing my face. Said Mark Traynor in February issue of *Cosmopolitan:* "First I decided on a woman's *type*. Is she high fashion? Is she pretty-pretty? Does she have a Florentine nose? Even if I can't make a woman beautiful, I can make her *interesting*." But I *am* interesting, Mark Traynor. It's *beautiful* I want to be.

Am writing article to go with makeover. What a relief. When Before picture is printed, I can write, "I never looked that bad." Am even considering having hair done for Before picture. "That," said my husband, "is like cleaning the house before the maid comes." Actually, I do that too.

Tuesday

Went to big noisy flashing psychedelic party tonight where told forty-five people *Cosmopolitan* making me over. All said it was great. Forty-sixth person said he liked me the way I am.

Wednesday

Before picture being taken today. Up at seven a.m. Washed hair. Set hair. Sat under dryer with moisture cream on face. Combed out hair. Applied make-up base and eye make-up. Put on favorite dress with openwork stockings. Flung open door at eleven a.m. to welcome Beauty Editor and Photographer. "This is me without any make-up," I said. Beauty Editor looked distressed. "You don't look bad enough," she said. "Do you have a bobby pin?" Curses. Had one. Beauty Editor pinned back hair in horribly unflattering style. Photographer began shooting.

"I feel I must tell you," I told him, "my left eyelid droops."

He looked. "Right," he said, and went on shooting. And shooting. And shooting. Me *au naturel*. Me less *au naturel*. Me inside. Me outside. Beauty Editor, having pondered how to make me over, reached decision. "You have a good daytime look," she said. "Maybe we should try for a nighttime look, for a glamorous new you." Yippee! A glamorous new me.

Everett and Cathy over for dinner. Told them this would be the last they would see of old unglamorous me and my good daytime look. "You mean," asked Everett, "that now you're Before and tomorrow night you'll be After?" Yes, said

I, smugly. "That's great," he said, "because at least there won't be any During."

DURING

Thursday

The big day for the new me. Arrived Lupe's ten a.m. Beauty Editor and Photographer waiting. Lupe appeared: boyish, Spanish, Pierre Cardin suit, Gucci shoes, solid-gold scissors. "What we are doing now," he said, "is de ringlets in de front and de shaggy in de back."

"Oh," I said.

"We are doing this now," he went on. "De ringlets in de front and de shaggy in de back. That is what we are doing. Now."

Had vision of everyone in high society marching up Madison Avenue with their ringlets in the front and their shaggy in the back. Did not want to be left out of trend. "If I do this," I asked, "how long will it take to grow back to where it is now?"

"Two years," said Lupe.

Decided to go for modified version: ringlets in the front but no shaggy in the back. Hair washed, snipped, set, dried in three hours. Am whisked into taxi by Beauty Editor and Photographer and taken, hair in rollers, to photographer's studio. Mark Traynor waiting: fortyish, carrot-haired, red-coated, satchel in hand. "Well," I said when we met, "am I high fashion? Am I pretty-pretty? Do I have a Florentine nose?"

"You're certainly not pretty-pretty," said Traynor, looking

critically and frowning. "Is this your regular make-up?" he asked. It was. Satchel unpacked. Out fell nine brushes, ten lipsticks, two sets false eyelashes, twenty-four bottles, twelve cakes eye shadow, powder, mascara, blush-on, eye liner. "I didn't bring my entire kit," he said, "but twenty-five different items should be enough for you."

"I feel I must tell you," I told him, "my left eyelid droops."

He looked. "Right," he said.

Beauty Editor explained to Traynor that layout would be in black and white. Traynor began. Told me my face too narrow, eyebrows too arched, chin too long. Told me he would widen face, de-arch eyebrows, shorten chin. "Of course, you could always have plastic surgery on your chin," he added. "Now, I had a friend with a long chin who had his chin broken in surgery and shortened. He looked *fabulous*. Just *fabulous*. Of course he died." Traynor applied base, plucked eyebrows, brought out bone structure with shadowing, lightened outside of face for widened effect. Put brown eye shadow on chin bottom to shorten, light line down nose to narrow, powder on eyebrows to de-emphasize. Throughout told rollicking tales of other lucky women he had made up and insulted. "The other night," he said, "I was at a beauty clinic on Staten Island and a girl who had freckles under her eyes asked me what I thought of using skin bleach to lighten them. I said I didn't know what product she was using, but that it was probably bad for her since the area under the eyes has so little natural moisture. Well, after I said that, her mother stood up and disagreed. She said she'd been using the same bleach for almost forty years. 'And, Madam,' I said, 'the skin under your eyes looks just like crepe.'" Traynor giggled with glee.

Then, still chortling, he tackled eyes. "Each eye is great," he said. "Individually." Painted, shadowed, eyelined, glued on false eyelashes. Put on bright red lipstick. "I have to for a black-and-white picture," he said. He looked into mirror. "Omigod," he said. "She's gorgeous." False eyelashes did not look false. Eyelid no longer drooped. Face was wide. Chin was short. Nose was narrow. "You look just like Kay Kendall," said the Beauty Editor.

"And remember," said Traynor, "you can't kiss anyone because half your face will fall off." He looked at my hair, still in rollers, and continued. "I know just how I would do your hair."

"How?" I asked.

"Very architectural and geometric and sculptured and short," he said.

"Really?" I said. "I always thought my hair should soften my features."

"My dear," said Traynor, "it's like putting a Rubens frame on a Picasso painting. You just can't put something that's soft and pretty around something that just isn't."

He paused. "Whoops. What have I said?"

Beauty Editor produced fluffy white-lace dress cut low and dangly earrings. Put them on. Traynor applied cleavage (brown eye shadow again). Lupe arrived to comb out hair. First hairdo soft, fluffy, and fortiesish. Loved it. Looked just like Gene Tierney. Looked luscious. Looked beautiful. Mark Traynor hated hairdo. Lupe hated make-up. I am not paying attention. I am overwhelmed. "It is," I announced, "no longer necessary for me to have a personality." Second hairdo: the ringlets in the front. Loved it. Looked just like Elizabeth Taylor. Mark Traynor hated hairdo. Lupe continued to hate face. "It's overdone," said Lupe. "But it had to be overdone,"

Beauty Editor explained to him, "because the pictures are black-and-white." Third hairdo: long ringlets everywhere. Loved it. Looked just like Scarlett O'Hara. Fourth hairdo: simple, just a few ringlets. Love ringlets. Husband arrived for inspection. He looked puzzled. "You look very strange," he said. "You look artificial."

"But it has to be this way," I said, "because the pictures are black-and-white. And anyway, don't you think I look like Gene Tierney?"

Finished photo session at six p.m. Took off fluffy white-lace dress and put it back in box to be returned to wholesaler. Took off earrings and dropped them into jewelry case belonging to wholesaler. Took off ringlets and put them back into wig case to be returned to wholesaler. Went home with my husband and my new face to my new glamorous life.

AFTER

Thursday Night

Husband and I arrived home. "I still think you look strange," he said. Began packing for trip to Mexico. Teen-aged sister, Amy, arrived to learn how to feed cats. "What did they do to you?" she asked. "It had to be this way for black-and-white pictures," I explained.

Girl friend Roz came over. "You look forty years old," she said.

"But," I protested, "I look just like Gene Tierney."

"Nevertheless, you look forty years old."

Went into bathroom and looked in bathroom mirror.

What a shock. Bathroom mirror looked nothing like little stage mirror I had sat in front of all day. Face in bathroom mirror looked nothing like face in little stage mirror I had seen all day. Face in mirror *did* look forty years old. False eyelashes looked as if two skunks were sitting on eyelids. Face looked buried under two feet of pink grease. Eye shadow on chin looked like five-o'clock eye shadow. "And why is your lipstick so red?" asked Roz. I began mumbling. "Gene Tierney . . . black-and-white pictures . . . had to be." Then I took out the cold cream and took off a little bit of the make-up.

"Now," said Roz, "you look only thirty-eight."

While leaving restaurant later that night bumped into Everett and Cathy. They began laughing. "You looked better before," said Cathy between snorts. "You look During," said Everett. I rushed home to cold cream and took off every bit of the glamorous new me.

Friday

Old me back in mirror. Ringlets have lost curls. False eyelashes sitting in medicine cabinet. Depression lifting. Mystery remains. For years I have been reading about makeovers in magazines. I would look at the new girl, made over top to bottom, and would think, 'Fantastic. That girl will *never* wear brown shoes with a black purse again.' What I did not realize is that when the pictures are over, the dress goes back to the wholesaler, the new hairdo goes back to the wigmaker, the new face disappears with the first night's cleansing, and you are left with two false eyelashes in the medicine chest, one tube of false-eyelash glue, and your brown shoes and your black purse.

Not that I didn't learn a great deal: I know how to widen my face, shorten my chin, and narrow my nose. I learned how to put in cheekbones where none had been. I learned that the make-up designed for a black-and-white photograph is not necessarily make-up designed for nighttime wear. But when it was all over, I did not look like Faye Dunaway. Or Kay Kendall. Or Elizabeth Taylor. Or Scarlett O'Hara.

Monday

MRS. DAN GREENBURG

LAS BRISAS HOTEL

ACAPULCO, MEXICO

PICTURES GOOD. YOU LOOK LIKE GOYA PRINCESS.

MALLEN DE SANTIS, BEAUTY EDITOR

And I didn't look like a Goya Princess, either. I looked exactly like Nora Ephron used to look. Only a little teeny bit better.

Women's Wear Daily
Unclothed

Women's Wear Daily *threatened to sue* Cosmopolitan *when this article appeared. Which I consider praise indeed.*

For any of you who are hanging by your Henri Bendel false fingernails as to what has happened to this merry little periodical since I wrote about it, I am told that it has gone right on giving hell to the Nixon girls, too much space to Jackie O., and orgasmic praise for the midi length. I wouldn't know myself, however. My subscription expired last year, I never renewed it, and I have been a better person ever since.

January 1968

Scene: The cloistered House of Balenciaga, 10 Avenue Georges Cinq, Paris, a fashion establishment so secretive about its operations it is often called The Monastery. Time: Just days before the Paris collections open. Enter a florist's delivery clerk, in shabby nylon dress and carpet slippers, delivering a bunch of flowers to Balenciaga's directrice, Mlle. Renée. Shuffling slowly through the salon, the clerk sees everything—the models, the collection, the look. She leaves with a two-franc tip. The following day, *Women's Wear Daily* prints advance sketches of the collection, its information supplied by the delivery clerk—a disguised full-time reporter for the famous newspaper of the women's clothing business.

Scene: Fifty-seventh Street, midtown Manhattan, half a block from Tiffany's. Time: Autumn, the clothes-buying season. Greta Garbo, New York's most elusive, least photographed celebrity, is window-shopping along the street when she is spotted by a *Women's Wear Daily* photographer. He begins snapping. Garbo runs, into one shop and out of another. The photographer stays in hot pursuit. He confronts her finally; she covers her face with her newspaper; he finishes shooting a roll of film. Next day, pictures of Miss Garbo hiding her face behind a copy of *Women's Wear Daily* run in the newspaper she has been hiding from.

Scene: The Massachusetts plant of Priscilla of Boston, the bridal-wear firm chosen to design Luci Baines Johnson's wedding dress. Time: July 1966, three weeks before the ceremony. A *Women's Wear Daily* photographer and reporter steal into the plant and search for Luci's dress. Days later

WW's celebrated preview sketch of Luci's gown appears; in retaliation, *Women's Wear Daily* is barred by the White House from the Johnson-Nugent wedding.

Women's Wear Daily is—through what its publishers think of as journalistic resourcefulness and its victims think of as dirty pool—the most ubiquitous, influential, snoopy, controversial, despised and adored publication in the fashion world. Whatever else *WW* may be, it is read, from front to back, by everyone in the business and thousands out of it.

Bill Blass, the Seventh Avenue designer for best-dressed women, who credits *Women's Wear* with his starburst success, picks up the paper every day on his way to work. Betsey Johnson, the miniskirted whiz behind the Paraphernalia boutiques, doesn't like *WW* at all but thumbs through it before chucking her copy into her psychedelic trash can. To Jacques Tiffeau, the widely acclaimed French-born designer, *Women's Wear* "is a marvelous meal every day. They know what's happening... the only newspaper in the fashion world that responds. But then, they're the only fashion newspaper." To Eleanor Lambert, the fashion publicist who originated the American Best-Dressed List, *Women's Wear* is "too personal, too collegiate, too juvenile, particularly in its crushes and enthusiasms. It picks on people. It isn't editorially sound, but it's journalistically brilliant. Of course I read it!"

John Fairchild, current head (and grandson of the founder) of the publishing empire that owns *Women's Wear*, is the man credited with *WW*'s immense notoriety and growing success. Fairchild is not surprised by the controversy created by his publication. "When anybody writes the inside story about fashion, he's bound to be unpopular," says the publisher.

The animosity that Fairchild and his opinionated journal have stirred up in the fashion world is an indication of, as well as a result of, the immense power that *Women's Wear* wields, a power far out of proportion to the paper's actual circulation. For one thing, *Women's Wear* is without competition in the trade; for another, because it is a daily, its news is six to eight weeks ahead of the monthly fashion magazine. A tabloid newspaper with a readership of over sixty-five thousand (who pay twenty dollars a year to subscribe), *Women's Wear* is *the* major fashion influence in the United States today, the oracle that states whether women will be wearing sackcloth, ashes, buttons, bows, buckles, chains, vinyl, or nothing at all from the waist up next year.

"We use *Women's Wear* as an extra pair of legs and eyes," says Henri Bendel's young president, Geraldine Stutz. "If it reports a collection is worthwhile, we will look at it. If it damns with faint or no praise, we will look at it last, if at all."

When *Women's Wear* chose the delicate French word *"sportif"* to describe certain country clothes that were being shown one season, Seventh Avenue designers were so impressed by the term that they charged off and began making ensembles guaranteed to make any American woman look as if she were auditioning to become Rex Harrison. Then, by the time the *sportive* look was ready to gallop into stores, complete with jodhpurs for ladies who did not ride and walking sticks for ladies who did not limp, *Women's Wear* abandoned the concept and announced that it was moving on to something called "the era of the gentlewoman."

Just what happened to the era of the gentlewoman is not clear, nor is anyone certain what will happen to other recent *Women's Wear* catchphrases like Prettygirl, Lankygirl, and

Realgirl. The *Raffinée* Look, coined for the refined clothes of some season or other, was dumped when *Women's Wear* publisher James Brady spotted something called the *Raffinée* Housedress selling for $2.95 in a Thirty-fourth Street bargain basement. "I came back to the office and announced that *Raffinée* was out," said Brady.

That its concepts arrive so quickly in the cemetery of old fads does not bother anyone at *Women's Wear*. "Fashion *is* change," says John Fairchild. And *Women's Wear* considers part of its function to nudge that change, spot the trends, push the merchandise. That *WW* has been wildly successful in performing this function has as much to do with its superb instincts as with the nature of the fashion itself.

"Elizabeth Hawes (one of the first great American *couturières*) once said that fashion is spinach, and no one has ever put it more accurately," said Leonard Hankin, vice-president of Bergdorf-Goodman. "The essence of what makes fashion news and excitement is hardly as clear as the science of building a skyscraper. You're not working with scientifically provable facts—we don't merely clothe the body, we clothe the spirit; we're enhancing the way a woman thinks about herself. As a result, if the average department-store buyer reads in *Women's Wear* that a certain collection is hot, he'll rush out to buy it. If, on the other hand, he buys what turns out to be a clinker, he can always remind the merchandise manager that he got the information from the 'Bible.' "

Designers are swept up in *Women's Wear*'s enthusiasms, too. "Look how few really creative designers and firms there are," says Deanna Littell, one of Seventh Avenue's most dynamic young talents, "just a handful. The rest of the industry cribs and copies any way possible. If *Women's Wear* tells

them to go see *Bonnie and Clyde*, there are some groovy
clothes in it, they'll all go see it and start making Bonnie and
Clyde clothes. I'm convinced the paper started a lot of
things itself: They gave tremendous impetus to the Zhivago
look, the Russian bit, and my God, *sportif*—that was John
Fairchild's biggest joke on the industry."

Women's Wear's writing style meshes perfectly with its
messages: It is catty, breathless, loaded with shorthand expressions and non sequiturs. SENTENCES ARE CAPITAL-
IZED FOR NO APPARENT REASON AND SEEM TO
SNAP AND CRACKLE RIGHT OUT OF THE PAGE.
French expressions punctuate the prose, no doubt sending
many Seventh Avenue manufacturers thumbing through
French-English dictionaries. "Annie is not going to become
brisée by success," *WW* wrote of one unbroken French starlet
who had made it big. *"Les hotsies"* and *"Les locomotives"* they
christened two groups of fashion-conscious young women
who scamper through the paper regularly and whose every
activity, no matter how trivial, is detailed. *"Je m'en fous,"* said
an apparently blasé French actress in a recent interview, to
which *Women's Wear* retorted: "IF SHE DOESN'T CARE,
WHY DOES SHE BITE HER NAILS?"

Mixed in with this grab bag of French and frenzy is a
range of news catering to both the paper's private readers
(most of them upper-class WASPS) and industry sellers
(mostly middle-class Jews). For Seventh Avenue manufacturers, for example, *WW* prints lists of buyers in town, sta-
tistics on "pantihose" sales, or the latest word on fashions
for infants and children—sometimes described in such
cozy Yiddishisms as *boyela* and *boytshikleks*. For Fifth
Avenue ladies, there are pop-art headlines ("Pow, Zowie,
Zap, Wap, Zonk" ran one recent tribute to Yves Saint

Laurent); offhand irreverence (" 'KISS ME, FOOL,' CRIED WILLFUL LITTLE HYDRANGEA AS HER SENSUOUS FINGERS TOYED NERVOUSLY WITH THE WRITHING TENDRILS OF HER NEW WHITE BACK-TO-SCHOOL DRESS BY X BOWAGE INC.," read a headline for a children's dress sketch); and incidental information on a dandy place to go to avoid the overcrowded French Riviera (Dubrovnik, Yugoslavia), what to bring to Russia (your own hairdresser), and how to keep up with the Winston Guests (Cee Zee's beige mastiff has his hair done).

Although fewer than one-sixth of *Women's Wear* subscribers are consumers, they are unquestionably the most consuming consumers of fashion in the country. Jacqueline Kennedy once declared indignantly that it was impossible for her to spend thirty thousand dollars a year on clothes (she would have had to buy sable underwear, she said), but experts estimate that it costs each of The Ladies well over that figure to dress the way she does. Small wonder that *Women's Wear* delights in aiming masses of information at them. Mrs. Charles Revson of lipsticks, Barbra Streisand of records, Charlotte Ford Niarchos of automobiles, Mrs. William (Babe) Paley of broadcasting, and the Duchess of Windsor of abdications all subscribe. So do Mrs. Ronald Reagan of California, Mrs. Nelson Rockefeller of New York, and Mrs. Winthrop Rockefeller of Arkansas; also Alice Roosevelt Longworth, Gloria Vanderbilt Cooper, several Italian *principessas* with backgrounds too confusing to go into, and George Hamilton's mother. Gloria Guinness, who is married to the banking Guinness, has two subscriptions— one for her Palm Beach home, the other for Paris. Mary Lou Whitney of the horse-racing Whitneys says that when she is summering in the Adirondacks, *Women's Wear* is the only publication that arrives on time; she may not be up-to-date on what is happening in the world, but she knows what everyone wore when it happened.

The group that *Women's Wear* calls The Ladies began to read *WW* in 1960, when John Fairchild returned from Paris and began to write about them. The Ladies are those socially registered women who summer in Southampton, winter in duplexes on Park or Fifth Avenue, and make a career out of looking beautiful and having lunch—a full-time job, requiring an early rise and a packed day. One must plan one's dinner parties, go to one's sinister Hungarian skin doctor, have one's biweekly massage at Elizabeth Arden and one's triweekly combout or set at Kenneth's, lunch at one of five recognized places for The Ladies to lunch (as of now: The Colony, La Grenouille, La Caravelle, LaFayette, Le Pavillon). One must exercise at Kounovsky's, discuss one's charities, shop for one's perfect dress with the perfect label and status shoes (by Fiorentina), stockings (opaque), belt (gold chain from Saint Laurent), bag (Gucci), face (Estée Lauder), false eyelashes (Bendel's), and return home in time to greet one's hobby (the husband, who, more often than not, is an investment banker or stockbroker, and the children).

The Ladies, unlike the fashion industry, learned to love *Women's Wear*, and with good reason: before *Women's Wear* became the swinging newspaper it is today, it was not really chic to be a Lady. There was something a little embarrassing about just doing nothing and having lunch in between. Oh, there were the charities and the children to be sure, but The Ladies occasionally sensed there might be Something More. Then, with their glorification in *Women's Wear Daily*, their elevation to a pantheon of heroines built somewhere in John Fairchild's noggin, and their constant pursuit by *Women's*

Wear photographers, The Ladies suddenly relaxed and became quite content. *Women's Wear* had created a profession:
It was *enough* just to have found that divine little pendant
made from a Coca-Cola bottletop; *enough* to have thought
of using one of those wide French neckties on one's skinny
shirt; *enough* to have divined that what one really needed
drooping from one's hair at Truman Capote's gala was a single white begonia.

The Ladies subscribe to *Women's Wear* to read about
themselves, to find out what clothes they are buying and
what they should buy, what designers they will patronize
next, what restaurants are fashionable, where their friends
are this month and whom they are in love with. But there is
one more reason The Ladies read *Women's Wear Daily:* it
serves as their Surrogate Bitch. Delightful, delicious, delec-
table, and delirious the newspaper *is*, but it is also bitchy as
can be.

Why, remember the time *WW* printed that terrible pic-
ture of Lady Bird Johnson with the ironic caption:
"Welcome to the Best-Dressed List"? The Ladies had a
good giggle over that. And another giggle when *WW* cited
Princess Margaret for being "The individualist of 1965 . . .
the woman who proved fashion doesn't count." When Mrs.
Hubert Humphrey arrived at the Capitol to hear President
Johnson's State of the Union message, *Women's Wear* com-
mented, "That little old dressmaker is at it again." One of
The Ladies, Jean vanden Heuvel, was found wanting at the
opera: "Jean vanden Heuvel," snipped *WW*, "needs a new
hairdresser." Even Caroline Kennedy was singled out for
bitchery this past summer. "THERE IS NO QUESTION,"
wrote *Women's Wear*, "THAT CAROLINE DRESSES
MUCH YOUNGER THAN HER AGE. Her smocked-to-

the-waist dresses, her short white socks, her semifitted velvet-collared coats all point to another era. Today, ten-year-olds wear boldly striped knits, chain belts, bright tights. Said one executive of a New York store where Caroline's clothes are bought, 'The surprise is that Jackie dresses her like a little girl of six or seven. Perhaps Mrs. Kennedy wants to keep Caroline a little girl so that she herself will look younger.' "

"*Women's Wear,*" said Marian Javits, wife of the New York Senator, "is like having a morning gossip with a pal who has taste, who's a little bitchy, and who goes to all the parties, my dear. It never condescends, it judges all the time. It is a giggle, a bubble, fun, fun." It is, in other words, a surrogate bitch.

The evolution of *Women's Wear Daily* into a fashion oracle and surrogate bitch began in 1960, but its history goes back a good deal further. *Women's Wear Daily* was founded in 1910 by E. W. Fairchild, the son of a Dutch Reform minister who in 1890 started to print a trade paper containing the business news he picked up while selling homemade yeast cakes to grocery stores. The Fairchild Publishing Company, which now publishes nine newspapers including *Home Furnishings Daily*, *Drug Weekly News*, and *Metalworking News*, picked up considerably with the addition of *Women's Wear:* it was a newspaper that supplied exactly what the garment business wanted—news of latex futures, new trends in sewing machines, and indiscriminate reports on every collection from shoes to hatpins. "It was encyclopedic," said *New York Post* fashion editor Ruth Preston. It was also dull as denim. "It sat on every merchandiser's desk, unread indefinitely," said Leonard Hankin. "You got it because you were in the business but you never looked at it."

E. W. Fairchild was proud of his newspapers; he often said he would never allow editorial comment to appear in his pages. "Our job is to mirror the industry, not to lead it," he declared. When his son, Louis, began to assume editorial responsibility in the late 1930s, the paper continued to have minimal impact; its reporters were seated ignominiously in the back rows of fashion shows and shunted around to the service entrance for outdated press releases.

Louis Fairchild began training his son to take over the company when John was fourteen; a student at the Kent School, he spent summers as an errand boy in the company offices. After graduating from Princeton, marrying the former Jill Lipsky, and working at a retailing job that consisted, John claims, of ordering paper panties for bathing suit tryons, he went to work for *Women's Wear* as a reporter. In January 1955, at the age of twenty-nine, he was sent to head the Fairchild operation in Paris; before long, the leaders of Paris *couture* were referring to him as *le blouson noir* and wishing for the old days when *Women's Wear* could be ignored.

During his indoctrination years in Paris, Fairchild went to parties at Pierre Balmain's and learned to stand on one foot on a bottle of Dom Perignon 1947. He listened while Italian designer Simonetta told him her collection was inspired by the egg, and while Christian Dior told him, "Fashion is something of the marvelous, something to take us away from everyday life." He ran a long series of interviews with the grande dame of *haute couture*, Gabrielle (Coco) Chanel, who said, among other things, "I hate breasts that show" and "Anyone past the age of twenty who looks into the mirror to be pleased is a fool." He feuded with Balenciaga and Givenchy, calling them the Dullsville Boys and dubbing their collections Flop Art.

When he returned to New York to become *Women's Wear*'s publisher in 1960, Fairchild set about changing the publication from fashion's pariah to fashion's arbiter. He opened the paper up to jazzier layouts, surrounded the sketches—which are considered superb—with lots of white space, gave his staff the freedom to do what it wanted, and brought in bright new personnel. One of them, the late Carol Bjorkman (a beautiful young woman who died of leukemia in 1967) wrote a column that left its readers charmed and chuckling. "Le Grand Charles," she wrote of a de Gaulle press conference she covered, "appeared—in a gray double-breasted suit with huge lapels (I am sure he is right—he is too large for the Ivy League cut), white button-down shirt . . . enormous gold cuff links, and a sweet touch— A GOLD WEDDING BAND." Miss Bjorkman covered prize fights, political campaigns, and went to see David Rockefeller, whom she referred to as her friend at the Chase Manhattan.

Fairchild continued to print the hard news that kept the tradesmen reading, but he also began to run features about people who weren't in the business at all. The most popular pages in the paper, the photo layout on pages 4 and 5, soon were filled with the marriages of Connecticut socialites, polo matches of Long Island horsemen, the lunches of The Ladies. "The Ladies . . . Are . . . BACK," wrote *Women's Wear* in a typical chronicle, "to the endless rounds . . . the forever decisions: Where to shop, what to buy, what to wear, where to wear what, when to go, how to go, why to be there . . . and—Who With? BACK: To the favored noontime spas . . .

the Midtown Manhattan Muncheries. . . ." And printed next
to The Ladies' pictures were Fairchild's comments on their
clothes and ensembles: frequently, he would place large
white Xs over their pictures to denote fashion sins.

The days of editorial nonparticipation were over. "Burn
their asses," shouted Fairchild, as he stormed through the
Greenwich Village city room in his three-piece suit. His
face, which bears an oft-noted resemblance to Alvin the
Chipmunk, sparkled with glee when his staff members
treated fashion with the irreverence he himself felt. "We
want the staff to be themselves," he said. "We don't want
them to become part of the Fashion Establishment, which is
like an ingrown toenail. We want them to have a fresh eye
on fashion and treat it with a sense of humor." (Except for
his daily lunches with designers at the Midtown Manhattan
Muncheries, Fairchild leads a quiet life away from the
Fashion Establishment, with his wife and four children in
New Canaan, Connecticut.)

For its first exclusive, *Women's Wear* took on *Vogue* magazine in a scathing attack that caused *Vogue*'s publisher
Samuel Newhouse to cancel all his advertising in Fairchild
publications. It began to expose the public to the designers
behind Seventh Avenue clothes and give credit where credit
was due—not to the man whose money paid for the produc-
tion but to the man whose pencil determined the flow of
fashion. It divided the designers into Greats, Realists,
Classicists, Risers, and Giants and managed to infuriate all
but the Greats. Eventually, it angered the Greats, too, and
Women's Wear achieved the sure sign of success in the fashion world when it was banned from James Galanos's and
Norman Norell's collections for real or imagined causes.
Designers' collections were graded by *WW* like examination

papers; the marks often depended as much on designers' deportment—toward *WW*—as on their excellence.

Fairchild's policy was to get it first by any means necessary. He broke official release dates on press releases. He sent reporters scaling the walls of private collections. Once he instructed one of his male reporters to dress in leather jacket and boots and ride his motorcycle to interview a member of European royalty known for his penchant for boys. Designers who refused to go along with *Women's Wear* found their seamstresses receiving bribe offers for sketches and themselves the recipients of Fairchild retribution. Priscilla Kidder of Priscilla of Boston refused to give *Women's Wear* an advance sketch of Luci's wedding dress; her reward was contained in *Women's Wear*'s once-removed coverage of the wedding.

"There was Priscilla in front of the President . . . in front of Lady Bird . . . in front of Pat—and at one point her backside completely blocked the camera's view of Luci. All of this effort—just to carry the three-yard lace train . . . A keen-eyed Washington observer, very close to the White House, comments, 'I was interested to see how Priscilla was fawning over Lynda all during the reception.' "

When Mollie Parnis, who often designs clothes for Lady Bird Johnson, released sketches of several of Mrs. Johnson's clothes to a competitive publication, Fairchild struck back. One day Miss Parnis was lunching at Grenouille and asked that her table be moved to a quieter spot to accommodate her luncheon guests. As it happened, she was moved to a table next to the Duchess of Windsor. Next day, in *Women's Wear*'s column Eye, Miss Parnis was accused of moving in order to sit next to the Duchess.

If *Women's Wear*'s tactics of revenge seem sophomoric

and its methods of obtaining stories unethical, they seem delicious to the staff. "We're a throwback to yellow journalism," said Richard Atkins, Fairchild's publicity man, smiling. And James Brady, who has replaced Fairchild as publisher of *Women's Wear* while Fairchild has moved up to president of the company, practically boasts about a four-million-dollar libel suit *Women's Wear* incurred from Genesco, settled out of court when Fairchild publicly apologized for several errors. "That was a good one," says Brady. He is blasé about *Women's Wear*'s penchant for stretching the truth of *Women's Wear*," he said. And he is right about that: the inaccuracies range from minor facts or dates wrong to major flubs (*WW* once printed an obituary of a man who had not died) to gross *faux pas*—such as *Women's Wear*'s page-one explanation of the 1965 power blackout. Rumor had it, the paper reported, that a "test of a revolutionary weapon to destroy enemy missiles" had deliberately drained the Northeast of power. "We overplayed it," said Fairchild later, in something of an understatement.

What really propelled *Women's Wear* into national prominence was a phenomenon that had nothing to do with its bickering with the Fashion Establishment. When Jacqueline Kennedy became First Lady in 1961, *Women's Wear* scrutinized, recognized and publicized every thread she wore, and Mrs. Kennedy unwittingly provided the paper with scoop after fashion scoop. At one point, she grew so weary of *Women's Wear* that, when asked if she read it, Mrs. Kennedy replied, "I try not to."

The First Lady's return to civilian life has not daunted her friends at Fairchild. Almost every purchase she makes is reported and usually applauded. "It's the casual Jackie," went one recent article, "that calls Paraphernalia, orders the Bush

Blouse in blue. Will she wear it with her new gold chain belt? Her Gucci shoes? And maybe pull everything together with a suède skirt, knee socks ... even pull her hair back with a signature scarf?" Tune in tomorrow for the solution to these pressing questions.

In December 1966 John Fairchild spotted Mrs. Kennedy at lunch at LaFayette in an above-the-knees skirt. He called his office, which in turn signaled a photographer who travels with an electronic bleeper device in his pocket for just such emergencies. The photographer rushed to the restaurant and snapped the picture that was reprinted in nearly every American publication. "Jacqueline Formidable," said *Women's Wear* commemorating the raised hemline.

Women's Wear's relationship with the White House has withered considerably during the Johnson years. It called Mrs. Kennedy Her Elegance. It calls Mrs. Johnson Her Efficiency, and her clothes are seldom applauded and only reluctantly. "The First Lady of the United States can, within reason, wear whatever she chooses," *Women's Wear* wrote tartly of one of Mrs. Johnson's recent appearances. "Thursday she did."

Lynda Bird Johnson is referred to as Lovely Lynda—LL for short—and the term has a distinct edge of sarcasm. *Women's Wear* could be pleasant enough to Miss Johnson, particularly during what it considers her Golden Age—the months she was escorted by Gorgeous George (GG). But when Miss Johnson announced her engagement to Marine Captain Charles Robb *Women's Wear* began to fret about her future as clotheshorse. Shortly thereafter, it published a devastating series of photographs entitled "The Metamorphosis of Lynda Bird," which prominently displayed several pictures taken before the ugly duckling became a swan. "George Hamilton may never go to Vietnam," wrote *Women's Wear* in crediting him with the transformation, "but he has done his bit for his country." But the future looked grim to *Women's Wear*, which asked: "NOW WILL LYNDA CONTINUE TO FLUTTER THOSE LOVELY WINGS? OR WILL SHE SLIDE BACK INTO PROVINCIAL ATTITUDES? She's certainly come an amazing way in just two years. With George's help, of course. And now it's up to the Marines. Will Chuck get the message across to her about those cheap accessories? Will he find her a good shoemaker?"

LL, GG, Her Efficiency, and Her Elegance made regular appearances in *Women's Wear*, along with an extensive supporting cast that includes Gloria Guinness (The Ultimate), Happy Rockefeller (Her Happiness), Princess Margaret (Her Drear), Ohrbach's head buyer Sydney Gittler (The King), Balenciaga (The Monk), and, of course, The Ladies— Babe (Paley), Amanda (Burden), Chessy (Rayner), Didi (Auchincloss), Pamela (Zauderer), Linda (Hackett), Isabel (Eberstadt), and Judy (Peabody)—all of whom John Fairchild has favored at one time or another for one reason or another. "I sometimes wonder," mused designer Bill Blass, "if we'd ever have heard of Isabel and Chessy and Didi if it weren't for John."

The Ladies themselves are rather fed up with the whole business. "At first it was flattering," said Judy Peabody. "After all, what woman doesn't like to think she's pretty?" But after a while, it got to be rather a responsibility knowing that whenever one went out a photographer might be lying in ambush. "There are times," said Mrs. Peabody, "when I would like to go out and not feel that I'm making an appearance."

(It must be noted, however, that whenever Mrs. Peabody is photographed by *WW* she smiles.)

And it must be further noted that, for its part, *Women's Wear* seems to be wearying of The Ladies. For one thing, The Ladies have begun to commit new and practically unforgivable fashion sins. "They'd rather be Socially Secure than Individual," lamented one recent article criticizing The Ladies for not wearing dark stockings and buckled shoes. "AREN'T THEY TOO YOUNG TO BE SET IN THEIR FASHION WAYS?" *Women's Wear*'s ambivalence toward The Ladies has been heightened recently: it ran a series of fictional adventures, written by one of their brightest young writers, Chauncey Howel, about two frigid postdebutantes named Didi Aubusson and Mimi de Nebbisch who take their decorators to lunch, shoplift at Lamston's for kicks, and behave in several other ways that may or may not be Ladylike.

In the last year, *Women's Wear Daily* has added fashion columnist Eugenia Sheppard. And its coverage of nonfashion events has broadened considerably. It prints articles on poverty, nuns' orders, the Vietnam black market, and dragqueen beauty contests; its art, movie, and drama critics have always been first rate—drama critic Martin Gottfried is nationally recognized. And when reading *Women's Wear* for its criticism is a little like reading *Playboy* for its fiction, there nevertheless are indications that *WW* is making a real attempt to place fashion in a slightly larger context. Despite the improvements, however, serious members of the fashion business wish that *Women's Wear* would concentrate more of its efforts on being at least accurate, at least ethical, at least mature, at least responsible—traits that *WW* displays only on rare occasion.

If *Women's Wear Daily* were writing about politics, its failings would be reprehensible. As it is, they are at worst, a *scandale*. For *Women's Wear* is, after all, only writing about fashion. AND FASHION, NO MATTER WHAT *WOMEN'S WEAR DAILY* SAYS, IS AFTER ALL, ONLY SPINACH.

Mush

"... there may be a new trend gathering momentum. It is a return to romanticism, a yearning for years past, when life was simpler and values stronger."

—TIME MAGAZINE

The media have been calling it a return to romance, but of course the return is only on the part of the media. The rest of the country never went away. The poems of Kahlil Gibran and books like *A Friend Is Someone Who Likes You* and *Happiness Is A Warm Puppy* have been selling hundreds of thousands of copies in recent years. Heart-shaped satin boxes of chocolate candy, single red American Beauty roses, record albums by Mantovani and the George Melachrino Strings, rhinestone hearts on silver chains—all of it sells to the multitudes out there.

What has changed, however, is that sentimentality is now being peddled by people who seem to lend it an aura of cultural respectability. Take Rod McKuen and Erich Segal. Both of them have hit the jackpot in the romance business: one is a poet, the other a professor. And each thinks of himself as much more than the mush-huckster he is. McKuen, the author of five slim volumes of sentimental poetry and countless songs, is the fastest-selling poet in America; Segal is the author of *Love Story*, which has sold almost 500,000 copies in hard cover, had the largest paperback first printing (4,350,000 copies) in history, and is on the way to being the weepiest and most successful film ever made. All of it is treacle, pure treacle, with a message that is perfect escapism to a country in the throes of future shock: the world has not changed, the old values prevail, kids are the same as ever, love is just like they told us in the movies. This optimism comes in nice small packages that allow for the slowest reader with the shortest concentration span and the smallest vocabulary.

To lump Segal and McKuen together here is not to say that they know each other—they don't—or that their work is alike. But there are some disarming similarities. Both appeal primarily to women and teen-age girls. Both are bachelors who enjoy referring to themselves as loners. Both belong to professions that rarely lead to commercial success. Both have the habit of repeating compliments others have paid them, and both do it in a manner that is so blatant it almost seems ingenuous. Segal, for instance, speaking on the prototype of his book's heroine: "JENNY exists and knows she is the inspiration for one of the strongest feminine figures in modern literature—honest to God, that's really what one critic wrote." Or McKuen: "There are a lot of people who take potshots at me because they feel I'm not writing like Keats or Eliot. And yet I've been compared to both of them. So figure that out."

More important, both of them have hit on a formula so slick that it makes mere sentimentality have the force of emotion. Their work is instantly accessible and comprehensible; and when the reader is moved by it, he assumes that it must be art. As a result, Segal and McKuen, each of whom started out rather modest about his achievement, have become convinced that they must be doing something not just right but important. Can you blame them? The money rolls in. The mail arrives by the truckload. The critics outside New York are enthusiastic. And to those who aren't, Segal and McKuen fall back on sheer numbers. Millions of people have read and loved their work. The stewardess on American Airlines Flight No. 2 from Los Angeles to New York loves every bit of it. "I'm so sick of all the crap in the world," she says. "All the killings, the violence, the assassinations. This one getting it. That one getting it. I don't want to read any more about that kind of thing. Romanticism is here to stay." She really said it. Honest.

I am a big crybaby. I want to tell you that before I tell you anything at all about Erich Segal. I cry at almost everything. I cry when I watch *Marcus Welby, M.D.* on television or when I see movies about funny-looking people who fall in love. Any novel by Dickens sets me off. Dogs dying in the arms of orphans, stories of people who are disabled but ultimately walk/see/hear or speak, having something fall on my foot when I am in a hurry, motion pictures of President Kennedy smiling, and a large number of very silly films (particularly one called *The West Point Story*) will work me into a regular saltwater dither.

One other thing about me before I begin. I love trash. I have never believed that kitsch kills. I tell you this so you will understand that my antipathy toward *Love Story* is not because I am immune either to sentimentality or garbage—two qualities the book possesses in abundance. When I read *Love Story* (and I cried, in much the same way that I cry from onions, involuntarily and with great irritation), I was deeply offended—a response I never have, for example, with Jacqueline Susann novels. It was not just that the book was witless, stupid and manipulative. It was that I suspected that unlike Miss Susann, Segal knew better. I was wrong to think that, as it happened. I was fooled by his academic credentials. The fact is that *Love Story* is Erich Segal at the top of his form; he knows no better and can do no better. I know that now. I know that I should no longer be offended by the book. And I'm not. What is it that I'm offended by? Perhaps you will begin to see as we go along.

"Dear Mr. Segal: I realize that you are a busy man but I must tell you something that will probably make you inspired and honored. This past summer a very dear friend of mine passed away. She was seventeen and hardly ever unhappy or sad. Leslie had read your book. Not once but three times. She loved it so much. It was funny but everyone related Love Story *with Leslie. She cried and said the story was so beautiful and realistic. When she was buried a copy of your book was placed next to her. . . . I wish you knew her. She was so unpredictable. That's what life is. She had an instant heart failure, and thank G-d she didn't suffer. I hope you don't think I'm a foolish college kid. I felt any person who could capture young hearts and old must be sensitive to life."*

That is a typical letter plucked out of a large pile of mail on Erich Segal's desk. There are thousands more, from old ladies who say they haven't cried that hard since the Elsie Dinsmore books, from young girls who want to interview Erich for their high-school papers, from young men who have read the book and want to go to Harvard and play hockey and marry a girl who has leukemia. The mail has been coming in in sacks since about Valentine's Day, 1970 (*Love Story* was published ten days before). The reviews of the book were exultant. The movie is now on the way to being the biggest film in history. And what has happened to Erich Segal as a result of all this? "I always was the way I am," he says, "only I was less successful at it. The difference being that people used to think I was an idiot ass-hole dilettante and now—you can find a nice adjective." Yes, Erich was always this way, only now he is more so. You can find a nice adjective.

"Erich, Erich, you're so pale," shouts Mrs. Jessie Rhine, a lady from Brooklyn, as Erich Segal, the rabbi's son, signs an autograph for her and rumples his curly black hair and stubs his toe and rolls his big brown eyes. His aw-shucks thing. Mrs. Rhine loves it, loves Erich, loves his book, and she would very much like to slip him the name of her niece except that there is this huge group of ladies, there must be a hundred of them, who are also surrounding Erich and trying to slip him the names of *their* nieces. The ladies have just heard Erich give a speech to eleven hundred New York women at the Book and Author Luncheon at the Waldorf-Astoria. Robert Ardrey, the anthropologist, who also spoke at the luncheon, is hanging around Erich, trying to soak up some of the attention, but it does no good. The ladies want Erich and they are all asking him where they can get a copy of his speech.

Erich's speech. Erich has been giving his speech for months on the book-and-author circuit and he has found that it works. The audience especially responds to the way Erich's speech praises *Love Story* at the expense of *Portnoy's Complaint* and then rises to a crescendo in a condemnation of graphic sex in literature. "Have you any doubt," Segal asks the ladies, "what happened between Romeo and Juliet on their wedding night?" The ladies have no doubt. "Would you feel any better if you had seen it?" No, eleven hundred heads shake, no. "Fortunately," Segal concludes, "Shakespeare was neither curious nor yellow." Wild applause. Everyone loves Erich's speech. Everyone, that is, but Pauline Kael, the film critic, who heard an earlier version of Erich's speech at a book-and-author luncheon in Richmond, Virginia, and told him afterward that he was knocking freedom of speech and sucking up to his audience. To which Erich replied, "We're here to sell books, aren't we?"

The phenomenon of the professor as performer is not a new one: many teachers thrive on exactly the kind of idolatry that characterizes groupies and middle-aged lady fans. Still, there has never been an academician quite as good as Erich at selling books, quite as . . . you can find a nice adjective. He checks in with his publicists once or twice a day. Is everything being done that could be? What about the Carson show? What about running the Canby review again? What about using Christopher Lehmann-Haupt's quote in the ad? Is this anecdote right for Leonard Lyons? "I've been in this business fourteen years and Erich is the closest thing to what a publicist's dream would be," says Harper & Row's Stuart Harris. "All authors feel they have to make a publicity tour, but they don't know how to do it. Erich knows. He knows how to monopolize the time on a talk show without being obvious. *I* would know he's obvious, *you* would know he's obvious, but millions listening in don't know. So many authors don't know how to say anything about their books. They're shy. Erich knows how to do it without being blatant. He had to make a speech the week he was number one on the *Time* magazine best-seller list. He wanted to get that over to the audience, that it was number one, so he got up and began, 'I just flew down and made three stops. Every time the plane landed, I got off and went to the newsstand and bought *Time* magazine to see if I was still number one on the best-seller list.' The audience adored it."

We're here to sell books, aren't we? Yes indeed. And Erich knows that every book counts. One night in a restaurant, an out-of-town couple shyly approached Segal and asked him to autograph a menu for a neighbor who had loved his book. "Why a menu?" Segal asked. Because, the couple explained, it was all they had. "I'll tell you what," said Segal. "There's a bookstore around the corner that's still open. Go in and buy a copy of *Love Story*, bring it back, and I'll autograph that."

Erich has been around the country several times, giving his speech, talking about his book, never letting the conversation wander away from its proper focus. "My novel, *Love Story*, and Paramount's film of it mark, I believe, the turning point in the morals of the younger generation." Erich said that in New York several weeks after publication. Note how it is self-aggrandizing, but in the cause of public morality. Note how it is reassuring to older people. Note the way the name of the book is plunked into the sentence, along with a plug for the film and a plug for the film studio. Erich got so carried away with slipping these little factual details into his sentences that Jacqueline Susann, who is no slouch herself in the self-aggrandizement department, felt called upon to advise him against it. "Every time you mention the book's name," she told him, "you don't really have to add that it's number one on the best-seller list."

Exactly what has made *Love Story* so phenomenally success-ful is something of a mystery. There are theories, but none of them fully explains what happened. Yes, it makes readers cry. Yes, it has nothing whatsoever to do with life today and encourages people to believe the world has not changed. Yes, as Segal points out, the book has almost no description; people tend to read themselves into it. And yes, it has come at a time when young people are returning to earlier ways. As the critic for Yale's *New Journal* pointed out:

"Segal has perceived that the revolution we all talk of being in the midst of is in large part a romantic one, a move-ment not so much forward as backward, away from technol-ogy and organization and toward nature and people. . . . *Love Story* is a trick, a joke, a pun on those among us to whom an alliance with the fortyish-matron set would be anathema. Segal has tricked us into reading a novel about youth today that has little sex, no drugs, and a tear-jerking ending; and worse, he has made us love it, ponder it, and feel it to be completely contemporary. We are, deep down, no better than the sentimental slobs who sit under the hair dryers every Friday afternoon. It's all the same underneath. Segal has our number."

When *Love Story* was first published, Segal himself seemed to possess a measure of self-deprecation. He admit-ted that his book was banal and cliché-ridden. But as time went on, he began to relax, the self-deprecation turned to false humility, and he took his success seriously. He acknowledged in a recent interview that he might well be the F. Scott Fitzgerald of his generation. He says that he has been compared to Dostoyevsky. He claims that his novel is in the tradition of the *roman nouveau* developed in France by Alain Robbe-Grillet and Nathalie Sarraute. He implies that people who hate his book are merely offended by its success. When *Love Story* took off in France, he called an associate long distance and said, "We are no longer a movement. We are a religion."

Can you blame him? Can you honestly say that you would have reacted any differently to such extraordinary success? Three, four years ago Erich Segal was just another academic with show-biz connections. "I lived for the day I would see my name in *Variety*," he recalled. He was born in Brooklyn in 1937, the eldest son of a well-known New York rabbi who presided over a Reform synagogue but kept a kosher home. "He dominated me," said Segal. "From the time I was the littlest boy I wanted to be a writer. My mother says that when I was two I used to dictate epic dramas to her. I believe her. I used to dictate tunes to my music teacher. I was that kind of spoiled child. But I came from a nice Jewish family. What kind of job was it being a writer? There was no security. My father wanted me to be a professional person." Rabbi Segal sent his son to Yeshiva, made him take Latin, and insisted he attend night classes at the Jewish Theological Seminary in Manhattan after he finished track practice at Midwood High School in Brooklyn. "I was always odd man out," said Segal. "It is true that I ended Midwood as president of the school and won the Latin prize, but those were isolated. What kind of social life could I have had? I spent my life on the subway."

At Harvard, which he attended because his father told him to, Erich was salutatorian and class poet. He ran every year in the Boston marathon and ran every day to keep in shape—a practice he continues. He also wrote two musicals, one of which had a short run Off-Broadway, and performed in the Dunster Dunces, a singing group that often sang a Segal original, *Winter is the Time to Snow Your Girl*. Despite his activity, he always reminded his friends not of Larry Hart but of Noel Airman. (The influence of *Marjorie Morningstar* on Jewish adolescents in the 1950s has yet to be seriously acknowledged.)

Segal got his Ph.D. in comparative literature and began teaching at Yale, where no one took his show-business talk much more seriously than they had at Harvard. Yes, Erich was collaborating with Richard Rodgers, but the show never got off the ground. Yes, Erich had a credit on *Yellow Submarine*, but how much of that was writing anyway? And then came *Love Story*. Script first. Erich's agents didn't even want to handle it. Howard Minsky, who decided to produce it, received rejections from every major studio. Then Ali McGraw committed herself to it, Paramount bought it, and Erich started work on the novel, the slender story of a poor Catholic girl named Jenny who marries a rich WASP named Oliver and dies after several idyllic, smart-talking, poverty-stricken years.

Not a single eye was dry, everybody had to cry. Even Erich Segal burst into tears when he wrote it. "In this very room," Segal said one day in his living room at Yale, "in that very chair at that very typewriter. When I got to the end of the book, it really hit me. I said, 'Omigod,' and I came and sat in that very chair and I cried and I cried and I cried. And I said to myself, 'All right, Segal, hold thyself. Why are you crying? I don't understand why you are crying. When was the last time you cried?' And I said, 'The only time I've cried in my adult life was at my father's funeral.' Now it's stretching a lot to make any kind of connection whatsoever. So I finally concluded, after all the honesty I could muster after forty-five minutes of crying and introspection, that I was crying for Jenny. I mean, I really was crying for Jenny. I got up and wiped my face and finished the thing."

Segal's apartment, in a Saarinen-designed dormitory, is a simply furnished, messy one filled with copies of *Variety*, unopened mail, and half-packed suitcases—Segal is rarely at Yale more than three or four days a week. He spends the rest of his time on promotion tours or in conference in Hollywood. (Two other Segal scripts have been produced: *The Games*, about marathon runners, and *R.P.M.*, about a campus revolt.) His icebox has nothing in it but yogurt, and Segal is relaxing in his living room, eating a container of the stuff and saying that he is happy with the lecture on *Phaedra* he delivered that morning because it convinced one of his students that Hippolytus was in fact a tragic hero. Student opinion of Segal at Yale ranges from those who dislike his book and his huckstering to those who rather like it and envy him for his success in what is referred to in cloistered environments as the real world. But most agree that whatever failings Segal has as a personality are overcome by his ability as a teacher. He teaches classics with great verve—in suede pants, he paces back and forth onstage, waves his hands, speaks quickly, gulps down a cup of coffee a student has given him, and generates enormous excitement. Segal has written several scholarly works, one a book on Plautus called *Roman Laughter*.

"It's a tremendous relief to be able to walk into a classroom and speak freely," Segal is saying. "I don't mean your mind. I mean your vocabulary. I don't go in for Buckleyish sesquipedalian terms, but I do go in for *le mot juste*. Even to be able to say, 'Aristotelian catharsis'.... On a podium, if I said that, they'd say who is this pompous bastard. This to me is a normal way of speaking. This is the existence whence I emanate. This is the way I really am." But if this is the way you really are, Erich, who is that traveling around the country delivering those speeches? And why?

"What am I going to say to them?" he replies. "I don't know. I had to sell books. I mean, do you know what I mean? I'm embarrassed but I'm not sorry, because the end justifies the means, you know. Three or four *yentas* who buy the book will get it to the readers who have never bought a book before, and get the readership I really cherish, which is the readership of the young people." He paused. "Do you think I was pandering to them?"

No. Not really. Because Erich Segal really believes in what he is saying, is really offended by sex in literature, is really glad he wrote *Love Story* instead of *Portnoy's Complaint*, thinks that—however accidentally—he has stumbled onto something important. Don't be fooled by the academic credentials: a man who can translate Ovid cannot be expected to know better—or know anything at all, for that matter—when it comes to his own work. "You see, I wrote the book in a kind of *faux naïf* style," Segal explained. "And if you think it's easy to write as simply as that, well, you're wrong. But little did I know that I was creating a whole style that's perfect for the Seventies. Let's face it. Movies are the big thing now, and this is the style that's right for the age of—as McLuhan called it—electronic literature. Writing should be shorthand, understated, no wasting time describing things. I had no idea that I was solving the whole problem of style this way. But I like it. I'm going to keep it for all my other novels." Can you blame him?

It is a well-dressed, well-behaved group, this crowd of young men and women, lots of young women, who are waiting patiently in Constitution Hall in Washington, D.C., for the concert to begin. You won't see any of your freaks here, no sir, any of your tie-dye people, any of your long-haired kids in jeans lighting joints. This is middle America. The couples are holding hands, nuzzling, sitting still, waiting like well-brought-up young people are supposed to, and here he is, the man they've been waiting for, Rod McKuen. Let's have a nice but polite round of applause for Rod, in his Levi's and black sneakers. You won't see any of your crazy groupies here, squealing and jumping onstage and trying for a grab at the performer's parts. No sir. Here they are not groupies but fans, and they carry Instamatics with flash attachments and line up afterward with every one of Rod's books for him to autograph. The kids you never hear about. They love the Beatles, they love Dylan, but they also love Rod. "He's so sensitive," one young man explains. "I just hope that he reads a lot of his poetry tonight."

They want to hear the poetry. They gasp in expectation when he picks up a book and flips it open in preparation. And onstage, about to give them what they want in his gravelly voice ("It sounds like I gargle with Dutch Cleanser," he says), is America's leading poet and Random House's leading author. "I've sold five million books of poetry since 1967," says Rod, "but who's counting?" As a matter of fact, Random House is counting and places the figure at three million. Nevertheless, it is a staggering figure—and the

poetry is only the beginning. There are records of Rod recit-
ing his poetry, records of Rod's music, records of Rod singing
Rod's lyrics to Rod's music, records of Rod's friends singing
Rod's songs—much of this on records produced by Rod's
record company. There are the concerts, television specials,
film sound tracks and a movie company formed with Rock
Hudson. There are the Stanyan Books, a special line of
thirty-one books Rod publishes and Random House distrib-
utes, with *Caught in the Quiet* its biggest seller, followed by
God's Greatest Hits, compiled from the moments He speaks
in the Bible. McKuen's income can be conservatively esti-
mated at $3,000,000 a year.

That literary critics and poets think nothing whatsoever
of McKuen's talent as a poet matters not a bit to his follow-
ers, who are willing to be as unabashedly soppy as their bard
and are not, in any event, at all rigid in their distinctions between song lyrics and poetry. "I'm often hit by critics and accused of being overly sentimental," Rod is saying to his
concert audience. "To those critics I say tough. Because I
write about boys and girls and men and women and summer
and spring and winter and fall and love and hate. If you don't
write about those things there isn't much to write about."
And now Rod will read a poem. "This poem," he says, "is
about a marvelous cat I once knew. . . ."

McKuen's poetry also covers—in addition to the subjects he lists above—live dogs, lost cats, freight trains, missed
connections, one-night stands, remembered loved ones and
remembered streets, and loneliness. The poem about the cat,
which is among his most famous, concerns a faithful feline
named Sloopy who deserted McKuen after he stayed out
too late one night with a woman. Her loss brings the poet to
the following conclusion: *"Looking back/ perhaps she's been/*

the only human thing/ that ever gave back love to me."
McKuen's poetry, which he reads to background instrumental accompaniment, is a kind of stream-of-consciousness free verse filled with mundane images ("raped by Muzak in an elevator," for example) and with adjectives used as nouns ("listen to the warm," "caught in the quiet," etc.). A recent McKuen parody in the *National Lampoon* sums up his style as well as anything; it begins, *"The lone$ome choo choo of my mind/ i$ warm like drippy treacle$/ on the wind$wept beach."*

Occasionally McKuen can be genuinely piquant and even witty. *"I wrote Paul this morning/ after reading his poem,/ I told him*, it's okay to drop your pants/ to old men sometimes/ but I wouldn't recommend it/ as a way of life. *I didn't mail the letter."* But for the most part, McKuen's poems are superficial and platitudinous and frequently silly. "It is irrelevant to speak of McKuen as a poet," says Pulitzer prize winning poet Karl Shapiro.

There was a time when Rod McKuen might modestly have agreed with Shapiro. Ten years or so ago, when he was scrounging in New York, living on West Fifty-fifth Street with Sloopy the cat and trying to make ends meet, McKuen might gladly have admitted to being just a songwriter. Even recently, after only two of his books had appeared, he told a reporter, "I'm not a poet—I'm a stringer of words." But then it happened: the early success mushroomed. "I don't think it's irrelevant to speak of me as a poet," McKuen says today. "If I can sell five million books of poetry, I must be a poet." Three million, Rod. "If my poetry can be taught in more than twenty-five hundred colleges, seminaries and high schools throughout the United States, if it can be hailed in countries throughout the world as something important, I must be a poet. In France, one newspaper wrote, 'Rod

McKuen is the best poet America has to offer and we should listen to him and mark him well.' "

The saga of Rod McKuen and his rise to the top is a story so full of bad times and hard knocks that it almost serves as a parody of such tales. Rodney Marvin John Michael James McKuen was born in 1933 in a Salvation Army Hospital in Oakland, California. His mother was a dime-a-dance girl; his father deserted her just before their son was born and McKuen has never met him. *"I remember hearing children/ in the street outside. . . . / They had their world/ I had my room/ I envied them only/ for the day long sunshine/ of their lives/ and their fathers./ Mine I never knew."*

McKuen's mother, Clarice, worked as a barmaid, scrubbed floors and operated a switchboard to pay bills. Then she married his stepfather, who drove tractors to level dirt for highways; the family moved from one construction site to the next in California and Nevada. "My stepfather used to get drunk and come home in the middle of the night and yank me out of bed and beat me up," McKuen recalled. "That was kind of traumatic."

At eleven, McKuen dropped out of school and went to work as a lumberjack, ditchdigger, ranch hand, shoe salesman and cookie puncher. At fifteen, he received his first serious rejection from a young lady. At eighteen, he became a disc jockey with San Francisco's station KROW, dispensing advice to the lovelorn. After a stint in Korea writing psychological-warfare material for radio, he returned to San Francisco and was booked into the Purple Onion. A screen test followed and in the mid-Fifties he worked at Universal on such films as *Rock, Pretty Baby* and *Summer Love*. In what must have been a move of some distinction, he walked out on the filming of *The Haunted House on Hot Rod Hill*. For his

film career, McKuen had a dermabrasian, which partially re-
moved his adolescent acne scars; he also has a long scar
across his chin, the result of an automobile accident.

In 1959 McKuen moved to New York and before beginning to compose music for the CBS Television Workshop, he
sold blood for money and crashed parties for food. Then in
1961, after the CBS job folded, he helped compose a rock
song called *Oliver Twist*, which was noteworthy mainly in
that it rhymed "chickens" with "Dickens." When no one famous could be found to record it, Rod did it himself; when
the record took off, he began touring the country with a
back-up group (he does not play a musical instrument and
has only recently learned formal composition). As Mr.
Oliver Twist he played Trude Heller's, the Copacabana
lounge, and did a twelve-week tour of bowling alleys around
the country. "He was a pretty big act," said his then-manager
Ron Gittman. "He wasn't your Ricky Nelson or your Everly
Brothers, but he pulled people." The constant performing six
nights a week proved too much for McKuen's voice: his vocal cords swelled, he could not speak, and after six weeks in
bed the old tenor voice was gone and a new froggy one had
emerged.

McKuen moved back to Los Angeles, played the Trouba-
dour, and continued to set his lyrics to the simple music he
composed in his head. In 1965 he opened at The Bitter End
and was praised by The New York *Times* and compared to
Charles Aznavour and Jacques Brel. Eddy Arnold, Johnny
Cash and Glenn Yarbrough began to record his songs of love
and loneliness. The market had changed. "In the Fifties
and early Sixties there were formulas," said rock publicist
Connie de Nave, who handled Rod when he was doing the
Oliver Twist. "Your group wore certain colors, sweaters over

pants, their hair had to be well-groomed, no smoking or drinking onstage. In the mid-Sixties suddenly the individual could wear what he wanted. He didn't have to spend $18,000 on arrangements for nightclub acts. All the outlets where Rod had to do the *Oliver Twist* died. The college market began. The change made things ripe for Rod. Before lyrics had been simple and uncomplicated. Now they wanted depth. No one could come out and go, 'Oo, wa, oo wa.' You came out with your stool and you sang, and you didn't even have to sing that great. You just had to feel. And as Rod was growing, the market came around."

Stanyan Street and Other Sorrows, McKuen's first book of poetry and songs, was an accidental by-product of a Glenn Yarbrough recording. When requests about the song began to pour into the record company, McKuen decided to publish a book containing it. With his own money, he paid for the printing, stored the books in his garage, and put the covers on and mailed them out in Jiffy bags. "I was very unsophisticated about it," McKuen recalled. "I didn't know what sort of discount you gave bookstores. I made them all pay cash and pay in advance. We had no salesmen, so I called the telephone company and got the yellow pages of all the major cities. We sent mailers to every bookstore. I knew people were asking for it and it wasn't listed in *Publishers' Weekly* or the guide to books. No one knew where it was from or how to get it." In a year, *Stanyan Street* sold 60,000 copies—about 120 times what the average book of poetry sells in a lifetime. Random House took over the distribution, signed McKuen to his next book, and gave him a Mercedes-Benz.

Today Rod McKuen lives in a thirty-room house on a hill facing Beverly Hills, which has a pool, orange trees, four in help, several sheepdogs and cats, and a barbershop for Rod and his streaky blond hair. He spends about half the year on the road and in Europe; he has an illegitimate son in France whom he sees frequently. When he is in Los Angeles, he rarely leaves his house except for a recording session or a trip to his office on Sunset Boulevard. "I have about fifteen people who work for me there," said McKuen. "I don't like to think they work *for* me. They work *with* me."

McKuen is sitting now in the music room of his house. He is wearing a yellow pullover sweater and the ever-present sneakers and Levi's and he is talking about the return to romance he feels the country is in the midst of. "I paved the way for Erich Segal," he says. "It's been my strange lot to have preceded all sorts of things for some time now. I told everybody that folk music was going to come in very big three years before it happened and nobody believed me and of course it did happen. And I went around telling people there was going to be a romantic revival and nobody believed that either. I think it's a reaction people are having against so much insanity in the world. I mean, people are really all we've got. You know it sounds kind of corny and I suppose it's a cliché, but it's really true, that's just the way it is."

It is not entirely easy to interview McKuen, you see. Not that he isn't open and garrulous—but for one thing, most of his thoughts seem to end up in statements he supposes are clichés; and for another he tends to ramble. Ask him about his childhood and within seconds he will be off on a ramble about prejudice and the Army. Ask him whether his poetry paints too sanguine a picture of the world and before you know it he will be telling you about capital punishment. Ask him about his new book:

"My new book has its roots in my childhood and in how

I feel now, about getting back to basics. You notice in this house, I like lumber. I like wood. Frank Lloyd Wright was my favorite architect because everything he did sprang out of the ground. And even though you see a lot of gadgets and stuff like that I like them because they are gadgets. They don't try to be anything else. I don't like artificial flowers, for instance. . . ." Like that.

In any case, it really doesn't matter to Rod McKuen how the interview goes, because he is sick and tired of being written about and criticized for what he is doing. Rod McKuen, who in the old days would talk to *Stamp World Magazine* if they wanted to profile him, has now become what he calls "gun-shy." Writers describe him as a guru and he hates it. Critics confuse his songs with his poetry and criticize him unfairly and he hates it. Everyone is out to get him. "You know, it's pretty fashionable to knock me down," he says. "There's something criminal, apparently, about being a successful poet. Too many writers take umbrage at that. It's not fair. I don't think poets should starve. I don't think anyone should starve. That's another problem we have in this country that should be changed. . . ." And off he goes on a ramble about poverty in America, leaving the reporter to wonder about it all.

What does it mean?

What does it signify?

What is McKuen trying to say?

And the answer is probably best put in a poem McKuen himself wrote: "*If you had listened hard enough/ you might have heard/ what I meant to say/ Nothing.*"

The Man in the Bill Blass Suit

Only one interesting thing happened to me as a result of this piece. A day after it appeared, a florist arrived bringing me a basket of flowers from Bill Blass. It was the hugest basket of flowers I have ever seen—and it was full of what I have always thought of as rich people's flowers: tulips, peonies, irises, roses, all of them out of season. They were beautiful. They took one look at my apartment and dropped dead on the spot.

December 1968

One day not long ago, Bill Blass, who is tall, slender, and tawny and speaks with a cigarette dangling from his lower lip, was standing in his brown plaid Bill Blass suit ($175), his brown Bill Blass shirt ($22.50), his brown Bill Blass silk tie ($15) and brown Bill Blass buckled shoes ($50) in the center of the Bill Blass men's *boutique* at Bonwit Teller's. A sign just outside the chrome-and-mirrored alcove announced that it was A DAY TO MEET BILL BLASS, and a few people came and did just that. Including:

A pharmacist from Cincinnati, who wandered in to say that he had found happiness in his maxi overcoat by Blass— "I was sick of getting my pants wet in the rain," he said—and that no one, not even the folks back in Ohio, thought he looked like a nut in it.

The dean of a Colorado business school, who said he was "tired of being in tired-looking clothes" and thereupon bought his fourteenth Bill Blass suit—a red plaid number with a snappy red checked tie to match.

A Sacramento real-estate man, who managed to drop twelve hundred dollars in less than an hour in the shop, some of it for two perfectly color-coordinated outfits recommended by the salesman, to be delivered with each item tagged with instructions as to what to wear it with.

The men's clothing business is currently undergoing its first substantial change in twenty years—since the World War Two veterans emerged from military uniform into the civilian uniform of the Ivy League suit. It is a change that has meant incredible revenues for manufacturers: in the last year alone, the number of suits cut is up seventeen per cent. It is a change that can count, among its virtues, the demise of the man in the gray flannel suit, white button-down shirt, and rep tie, and among its excesses, the Nehru jacket, the formal white turtleneck, the overuse of the word "peacock," and—yes, folks, it really happened—the manufacture of a pair of dotted Swiss see-through pants.

Two years ago, when the Hollywood hipsters and New York creative types zipped themselves up snug into Pierre Cardin's cosmonaut look, it might have been premature to call what was happening a revolution. But today, when the behavior of Cincinnati pharmacists, Sacramento realtors, and Denver educators is being affected, it is clear that the revolution has not only come—it is here for good, and settled firmly into a mellow period of consolidation.

The entry of women's-wear designers like Blass into the men's field is part of the industry's attempt to cope with demands of an affluent country for more clothes and fashion in clothes, a demand the men's-wear industry, a notoriously sluggish one, had nothing whatsoever to do with and seems somewhat puzzled by. Fashion, the expression goes, begins on the street (in this case, on Carnaby Street and St. Mark's Place), and most of the big men's-wear manufacturers seem to wish the new look had stayed there.

"They're hoping it will all go away," said Bill Blass, "and they can go back to making blue serge suits."

Blass first tried to get into men's wear ten years ago, and he was assured at that time that it was hopeless to change the way men dressed. "I spoke to a group of manufacturers," he recalled, "and they told me there were two minority groups that doomed every fashion development—the homosexuals and the Negroes. Acceptance by these groups supposedly made fashion unacceptable to the rest of the population. But things have changed. Another minority group—the young—changed everything. The young could wear the most effeminate clothes without being suspect in

the least. And the other minority groups have suddenly become acceptable."

Cardin was the first women's designer to plunge into
men's wear; he was soon followed by John Weitz, Hardy
Amies, Oleg Cassini, and, eighteen months ago, Blass. In that
short time, Blass clothes have become available in forty department stores; this year Blass labels will probably double
the 2.5 million dollars they grossed last year. "By now," said
Blass, "everyone's trying to get in and make a killing."
Designers are rushing in—among them Donald Brooks,
Jacques Tiffeau, Oscar de la Renta and Geoffrey Beene—
and manufacturers are frantically signing them up. A few
weeks ago Mike Daroff, president of the 140-million-dollar
men's wear conglomerate, Botany Industries, told a reporter
he thought the whole women's-designer-in-men's-wear
movement was just "a big fad and a lot of noise." Days later
he announced that he was hiring Dior's Marc Bohan to design a collection.

Bill Blass is no radical hero of the men's-wear revolution. Unlike Cardin, who, in addition to creating his space
suits, changed the shape of clothes to the fitted, updated
Edwardian look that now dominates the market, or the
Beatles, who managed to prove once and for all that dandy-
ism and homosexuality did not necessarily occur simultaneously in nature, Blass has done nothing dazzling or
extraordinary. The most explosive comment he makes about
men's wear is that ties will have to go—not this year, not
next year, but someday.

"The only important thing about the Nehru jacket is
that it opened up the possibility for the tie's disappearance,"
he says. "The wider tie has given the look a different dimen-
sion, but ultimately the tie will go. Men will use scarves or

something—a man needs something up around there to set his face off since he doesn't use cosmetics. At least, not yet."

His major policy statements are even less earthshaking: they concern subjects like brown ("Most men have brown hair and brown eyes and brown looks marvelous on them"), red ("Red is the most masculine color in the world"), and blue ("The blue shirt has been a boon to men with sallow complexions"). Although he has designed them, he does not think men will go all the way for maxi-length coats. On turtlenecks during the day, his view is: "Fine, in the country." On turtlenecks at night: "Out! Never in. The only time I was interested in the look was in Cleveland, where I saw an elderly gentleman wearing one. He must have been very unsure of it because he wore it with a bow tie. He had my sympathy." On he-and-she fashions: "Only for the young." On the possibility of an androgynous society: "Not in the near future." The nastiest remarks he makes are on the topic of the gray flannel suit. "I feel downcast in a gray flannel suit," he said, "and I see no reason for anyone to wear one unless he's a stockbroker or an undertaker."

What is significant about Blass, however, is that his clothes appeal to a group of men who have hitherto been resistant to fashion change—a group which, in fact, includes the stockbrokers and undertakers, who can well afford to pay the extra premium for colorful, well-tailored, tasteful clothes but want nothing to do with ruffled blouses and love beads.

"I think all that exaggeration of costume dressing and kinky fashion was tasteless but it was a phase we had to go through," said Blass. "Exaggeration isn't what I'm after. The crushed velvet pants, the coats from Tibet, the jewelry, which I find particularly vulgar, had to come out so that the poor drab gray-flanneled man would become aware that something had to change."

"One of the reasons Bill's clothes are so successful in towns like Dayton," said Bill Flink, who heads the Blass men's wear operation, "is that he's very careful about how far to go." Danny Zarem, head of Bonwit's men's department, adds, "Bill's done for the American-English look what Paul Stuart's men's show did fifteen years ago. Paul Stuart took an accepted traditional look and updated it. They took the natural shoulder jacket and did it in interesting fabrics. They took the rep tie, which had always been done in dull navies and burgundies, and kicked it up. In the same way, Bill's taken things men have always related to, like the English cut in suits and big bold Shetland plaids used in hunting jackets, and kicked them up without being silly. Everything he does smacks of country, breeding, and good taste."

Taste is the word you hear most often about Bill Blass. Bill Blass has taste. No question about it. Taste, of course, is an intangible thing, but some of the tangibles that make his taste so impeccable include twenty-five perfectly tailored suits, three dinner jackets (one of them lightweight for dancing, the others heavyweight for just plain eating), several dozen pairs of shoes cut for his very own feet by Lobb of London, and twelve overcoats, two of them fur-lined. He has a valet named Hugh who serves tea complete with watercress sandwiches. When he goes to London, he packs only his underwear; when he lands, he goes straight to his tailor—Kilgour, French and Stanbury—and picks up the five suits he ordered on his last trip abroad. Bill Blass has taste. Wonderful taste. Everyone knows it.

The women of America first began to hear of Bill Blass

and his wonderful taste about nine years ago, when he became head designer at Maurice Rentner, Ltd., a prosperous
Seventh Avenue house with a reputation for dressing the
amply-proportioned woman. "Our 1959 collection was
quite a shock to the buyers," Eugene Lewin, Rentner's chairman, recalled. "They came in looking for matronly stuff and
we gave them Bill's young look. It was like walking into a
steak house and getting a Chinese meal. They ate it up."

The Blass look for women was a luscious, soft, feminine
look for evening, with loads of ruffles and lacy dresses, and
an easy-to-wear, brilliantly colorful look for daytime clothes.
Blass was a sketcher, not a tailor; his strength lay in his color
sense—he became famous for combining checks with plaids
and stripes with tweeds—not in his notions on shape. "I
don't pretend to be a Balenciaga or a Courrèges," he said. "I
simply want to make clothes for now."

What gave Blass an extra boost in the fashion world was
the fact that before long he became a Beautiful Person. A
perennially suntanned bachelor who was good-looking and
utterly charming, he was the first of the fashion designers to
enter into what Marylin Bender has called "the marriage of
fashion and society." Blass, Miss Bender wrote in her book,
The Beautiful People, "has the relaxed posture of a man
whose major activity is clipping coupons." It is a posture he
manages to maintain while all those around him are buck-
ling under stress.

At the dress rehearsal this fall for the Coty Awards fashion show, where Blass received a citation for his men's wear,
he stood backstage during what was clearly a crisis and listened blandly as an assistant told him there was no black
shirt, no presser for the wrinkled suits, no tan sweater, no
wooden hangers, and the wrong size raccoon coat. "And

someone spilled mouthwash on the rain hat," Blass added
calmly. "Don't forget that." A few weeks later, just before the
press opening for his women's spring collection, Blass, cigarette drooping, leaned against the dressing-room wall at
Rentner while eleven models scrambled frantically for shoes.
"Can you imagine?" he said, smiling. "One hundred pairs of
shoes are not here." He chuckled. "Can you imagine?"

Blass broke Seventh Avenue tradition by inviting his private clients to press showings, and as the models appeared,
all the socially registered women *Women's Wear Daily* includes among the Ladies—Missy (Bancroft), Chessy
(Rayner), Mica (Ertegun), and Louise (Savitt)—would sit
and gasp and whisper and applaud and mark down the
clothes they wanted to order on long slips of paper. Then, at
night, Blass, the debonair extra man who always knew which
fork to use, would go to Missy's or Chessy's or Mica's or
Louise's, or they would come to his East 57th Street pent-
house and dine on the terrace among fifteen thousand dollars' worth of trees.

"It was quite a phenomenon when it first happened,"
said *Vogue* editor Carrie Donovan. "I remember saying to
Louise Savitt about five years ago, 'Louise, has he really
made it?' 'Yes,' she said, 'and I'll tell you something else. The
husbands love him, too.' "

Said Mrs. Savitt, a young divorcée Blass frequently es-
corts, "Bill's great thing about clothes was that he was the
first designer to go out and lead the social life." Another
friend, Missy Bancroft, who was a Blass model before her
marriage, agrees. "I used to work for some of the other designers," she said. "They'd never *been* to Morocco. They *never*
went to '21.' Their clothes fit *nowhere* into your life. Bill

knows exactly what you need to wear. He's been *every-where*."

Bill has not been everywhere, but it does seem that way. He went to Acapulco and Marrakech before one went to Acapulco and Marrakech. He has followed the bulls through Spain and he weekends on an island in Maine. Once, a few years ago, he and a friend named Jerry Zipkin (whom *Women's Wear* describes as Social Moth Jerry Zipkin) wanted to spend Christmas at a place they'd never been to and the only spot they could come up with was Miami Beach. Partly because of his extensive travels and partly because of a long-standing, somewhat uncontrollable Anglophilia, Blass occasionally speaks in a slight English accent. "He had an English phase," explains Mrs. Savitt, "and years ago, when I was working at *Vogue*, I was told Diana Vreeland had once asked someone, 'Tell me, what part of England is Bill Blass from?'"

As it happens, William Ralph Blass is from Fort Wayne, Indiana, where he was born under the sign of Cancer forty-six years ago, the son of hardware store owner Ralph Aldrich Blass and his wife, the former Ethyl Keyser. At the beginning of the Depression his father committed suicide; he and his older sister were raised by their mother. Following his graduation from Fort Wayne High School, where he played football and sketched for the newspaper, Blass left the Midwest for good—and fairly shudders when he thinks about it.

"Indiana?" he said. "It never happened. I never went back. It was for me almost as if the whole process of growing up was based on waiting until I could get out. Do you know, down the street from me had lived a girl named Jane Peters who ended up in Hollywood as Carole Lombard. As a kid, I thought of her as a straw in the wind. I thought, 'She got out. She made it. I can, too.' Look, Fort Wayne is probably as attractive a place for a youngster to grow up in as any other small American city, but what can I say? I didn't like it. I've known what I wanted to do since I was five years old. And you don't, if you have aspirations to design clothes, talk about it in a town of that size. I felt like a prisoner released when I came to New York."

Blass dropped in and out of Parsons School of Design shortly after arriving in Manhattan and went to work as a sketcher for David Crystal. Then he served for three years in the Army in a camouflage unit which included a number of artists who had volunteered, thinking they were in for a cushy enlistment. Instead, the unit was sent to Europe as a dummy decoy division. "It was a suicide mission," said photographer Art Kane, who was part of the unit. "Our job was to come in, with rubber tanks and recordings of battle noises, inviting enemy fire after a unit pulled out."

Blass still carries with him a cast-iron saltcellar owl he found while digging himself a foxhole during the Battle of the Bulge. Years later friends heard about it and—"Oh, my God, the owls I got for presents," he said. "I can tell you after a while they became anything but amusing." (In addition to his owl collection, Blass also has coffee tables full of netsuke tigers and horn cups and walls full of antlers and paintings, a few of them abstracts by Blass himself.)

If Bill Blass was ever a hick, no one can remember it. Even in his Army days, he had taste. "He wasn't a typical Hoosier," said graphic designer Ned Harris. "His uniform did not look like anyone else's uniform." There was a reason: a week after enlisting, Blass had taken his dress uniform to Brooks Brothers and had it altered to fit.

Following his discharge as a corporal, Blass worked as a sketcher for Anna Miller; then, when Mrs. Miller merged with her brother, Maurice Rentner, Blass went over as second designer. He is now vice-president of Rentner, which grossed 4.1 million dollars last year, and president of Bill Blass, Inc., a licensing firm that handles his business dealings with manufacturers who hire him to design luggage, swimsuits, men's wear, and other products. This year Blass's business manager estimates he will earn a quarter of a million dollars from his combined efforts.

In the early sixties, when designer names began to appear on manufacturers' labels and American designers became celebrities of sorts, Blass began making extensive public appearances around the country with his models and clothes. "He's a superbusinessman," says New York *Post* fashion editor Ruth Preston. "He can sell the eyelashes off a hog." Some of the other designers traveled, but few went at it as relentlessly as Blass. "Anyone's a damn fool to think it isn't important to go on the road," he said. "New York is not America. New York women are fickle about designers. But if Sarmi comes to Minneapolis and tells someone she looks sensational in green chiffon, that lady will be Sarmi's forever."

Several hundred thousand miles and three Coty Awards later, Bill Blass has become a household word—"Almost as well known as Dior," says Bonwit's president Mildred Custin. Nothing did as much for Blass as a series of AT&T advertisements, picturing a group of models in fluffy Blass dresses, surrounding the designer. The caption read, "Fashions by Bill Blass. The Trimline Phone at Your Bell Telephone Company."

Publicity seems to fall Blass's way without his lifting a finger: the AT&T people came to him; so did the Haig-Pinch bottle ads, showing a group of identified Beautiful People surrounding an unidentified Blass. And then there was the time when Jean Shrimpton posed for a Revlon ad in an antique white Chantilly lace dress by Blass. Minutes after the lipstick placard hit the drugstores, the Revlon switchboard lit up with calls from women demanding to know where they could buy the dress. Rentner sold sixteen hundred of them, at $160 and $225, thus making it the best-selling, most publicized dress in Seventh Avenue history.

Designing dresses, raincoats, swimsuits, luggage, furs and children's clothes might have been quite enough for most designers; not for Blass. "As busy as you can be with the women's thing," he said, "I felt it wasn't enough. I like making clothes, but I can't get emotionally carried away by them. Adolfo, who does the hats for my shows, told me that one designer was describing one of his dresses to him and burst into tears. And at the Coty Awards, I sat in front of one of the winners, and he wept right through the fashion show of his own clothes. I think that clothes are a very necessary part of our lives, but to get so carried away by them.... Anyway, I would work on Seventh Avenue and have hours empty."

Two years ago David Pincus, a Philadelphia men's-wear manufacturer who realized that women's-wear designers like Cardin were about to strike it rich in men's wear, decided to hire an American designer for his firm, Pincus Brothers-Maxwell (PBM). He asked his wife, his sister Sylvia, and several of his female cousins for suggestions, and the name that kept coming back was Bill Blass. Pincus went to see Blass, who agreed to a deal on the spot. "I had anticipated going into men's wear," said Blass, "and I wasn't nervous about it at all. It seemed like such a natural evolution for me. And after all, I knew something about men's clothes, if only from forty years of dressing myself."

The first Blass collection for PBM made its debut in June 1967, and except for one green plaid kilt, shown with a green velvet jacket, it was a smashing success. Blass called the show his getaway collection, and its strength lay in its English country suits, in windowpane plaids, that had a marvelous outdoors, masculine feeling. Bonwit Teller decided on the spot to build a *boutique* for Blass. "Without even seeing a Bill Blass collection, both Miss Custin and I knew he couldn't do anything bad," said Bonwit's Danny Zarem. "The way he dresses, his marvelous eye for color, shape, and fit—we could visualize just who he was designing for and what he would design."

Among the men who wear Bill Blass clothes are Senator Jacob Javits, William Paley, Mayor John Lindsay, William Buckley, and Kirk Douglas. But the typical man in the Bill Blass suit is an affluent suburbanite who once owned a Madras jacket, plays golf at his country club, drives a Thunderbird which he thinks is a sports car, and brings a bottle of liqueur back from the islands every February and makes all his friends drink it. "He's over thirty," said Blass. "He's tall, a little thick in the middle and heavy in the legs. He's apt to be a business type. Sounds awful square, doesn't he?"

Yes, indeed. The man in the Bill Blass suit does not want

to look silly—or worse, effeminate (the polite word he uses for homosexual). He wants to look with-it—which he does in his fitted, striped-checked Blass suit. He wants to feel secure—which he does when the suit is lined with silk covered with the Bill Blass double B insignia (the first B is printed backward) and buttoned with brass BB buttons. And he wants to look as if he had taste—which he does, his wife assures him, because Bill Blass was in town only last month, and *he* looked as if he had taste.

"I really believe the American woman is one of the reasons it's taken so long for anything to happen in men's clothes," said Blass. "Years ago you'd go out of town and see some dame who was voting for Nixon and she would tell you she didn't want her husband to wear anything but a navy-blue suit. She didn't want to lose control of him, and she was terrified that if he dressed in anything that might be construed as effeminate, people might see what the true nature of their relationship was.

"But now I find women have rallied to my side. It's the woman who says, 'Oh, Fred, go ahead and buy those red loafers. They'll be just wonderful in Boca Raton.' And when women go out at night in minidresses, they don't want their husbands to fade away into the background. They want their men to be part of the whole picture."

The Blass look for men is not without its critics. There has been widespread disapproval throughout the industry of Blass's use of signature linings and buttons. "To me," says one men's-wear manufacturer, "it's like sticking a $150 price tag on your lapel." *Women's Wear Daily*'s publisher James Brady conceded that Blass has a great color sense and good taste, but said, "He's not the most creative designer. He's never created a new shape." And George Frazier, the immaculately tailored *Esquire* fashion writer, thinks some of Blass's resort clothes are very so slightly effeminate—a charge Blass finds more interesting than accurate.

"Isn't this fear of looking homosexual a peculiarly American thing?" he said. "There's no group of men as vain as the Latins. Spanish men are immaculately tailored and each hair is perfectly combed. Even the bullfighter is as vain as any person can possibly be, but there's never any question of *his* masculinity. I suppose it's partly because the women in Latin countries have very little status, unlike American women."

The success of his men's line has done much to fill up Blass's empty hours. When he is in New York, he leaves for his Seventh Avenue office at nine a.m. in a rented limousine. His secretary, Sandy Price, is waiting with coffee, three packs of True cigarettes, and a stack of letters, a few from would-be designers seeking advice on how to break into fashion. At ten, the phones start ringing, and Blass begins the work day, choosing fabrics, fitting clothes for the next collection and seeing important buyers. Lunch, observed religiously from one to two-thirty p.m., is usually taken at one of the Three La's—La Grenouille, La Caravelle, or La Côte Basque—either with friends outside the trade or designers, like close friends Jacques Tiffeau, Norman Norell, and Oscar de la Renta, to whom Blass is "Bilbo."

After lunch, Blass returns to his office until four p.m., when he goes up to the men's showroom on West Fifty-eighth Street. At six, he walks ten blocks crosstown to his apartment, where the valet, a Scotch and soda, and a crackling fireplace are waiting. He may spend the evening out—at a small dinner party at Mrs. Gilbert Miller's, for example, or at the Horse Show—or he may order sandwiches from Reuben's for himself and a friend.

Such New York days are dwindling down to a precious few: in a recent three-week period, Blass went from New York to Minneapolis (to do a men's-wear show), to Chicago (for an Evening with Bill Blass to benefit a local hospital), to New York (to open his spring collection), to Maine (to spend a quiet weekend at his fishing shack), to Lancaster, Pennsylvania (to discuss watch design with the Hamilton people), to New York (to speak before the Advertising Women of New York), to Scotland (to pick the plaids for next year's collection), and to Italy (to consult with his shoe people). Not surprisingly, his friends think he is working too hard. "He has an image as a party boy," says fashion publicist Eleanor Lambert, "but three or four times a week he's simply home in bed, collapsed."

"If I didn't have the house in Maine, I'd probably blow my top," Blass said one night as he sat at home, collapsed, in front of his fireplace. "Your private life and your public life have to be separated. You cannot be all things to all people. You spread yourself too thin. I had lunch today with a client from San Francisco and she asked me if I minded traveling and talking to so many people. Actually, I find it interesting. But you do get tired of smiling."

But Bill Blass goes right on smiling that genial smile. The customers come into the store and dumpy men from Detroit slip into corduroy knickers, and Bill Blass smiles and tells them they look wonderful. Dumpy ladies in Atlanta come to meet him at Rich's and he smiles and they walk out with five dresses. Last year, he was even asked to design a tire. He turned it down, smiling. And jewelry. He turned that down, too. "I don't believe in jewelry for men," he said.

And there have been offers to design carpeting, wallpaper, fountain pens, sunglasses, and kitchen equipment—all of them rejected. "You have to evaluate those products very carefully," says Blass. "Do they fit in? Do they have validity for you? Kitchen equipment doesn't have any validity for me. But I'll tell you what I would like to redesign. American automobiles. Why shouldn't your convertible have a bold brown-and-white plaid upholstery instead of green brocade plastic? Why shouldn't sports cars have white linen slip covers in the summer time?" He paused and grinned. "I'll tell you this," he said. "I wish all those gray-flannel-suited men had their cars upholstered in gray flannel. It would look much better on cars than on them."

A Rhinestone in
a Trash Can

and *The Love Machine* Phenomenon
of J. Susann

I wanted to write about Jacqueline Susann for a couple of reasons: I think that anyone who can play such a colossal joke on the publishing business cannot be all bad; and more important, I think that her trash is better than it has been made out to be. Unfortunately, a number of other critics said this at about the time my article appeared, which took some of the perversity out of it.

May 1969

Robin Stone *is* the love machine. My goodness yes. Robin Stone, who drinks his vodka straight, who is positively insatiable in the kip, who runs the largest television network in

the country, and who is not only a magnificent sadist but a
weak and vulnerable one at that, is the love machine.
"I think Robin Stone is divine," says Jacqueline Susann.
"Don't you?"

Yes.

Robin Stone is, of course, the hero of Miss Susann's new
novel, *The Love Machine*, and if he has brought happiness to
almost none of Miss Susann's fictional heroines—who are,
incidentally, the most willing group of masochists assembled
outside the pages of de Sade—he is nevertheless on the verge
of transporting the book sellers of America to unparalleled
heights of ecstasy. Hot on the heels of Alexander Portnoy
and his Complaint (Philip Roth's novel now has a staggering
four hundred fifty thousand copies in print) come Robin
Stone and *The Love Machine* (with a first printing of two
hundred fifty thousand copies). And along with the book, as
an added dividend, come Miss Susann and her husband, producer Irving Mansfield, who have already begun the first of a
series of nation-wide tours dedicated to knocking Roth off
the top of the best-seller list.

"It's wild," said Michael Korda, editor-in-chief at Simon
and Schuster, which is publishing Miss Susann's novel. "You
have these two giant books out at the same time, and their
merits aside, one of them is about masturbation and the
other is about successful heterosexual love. If there's any
justice in the world, *The Love Machine* ought to knock
Portnoy off the top simply because it's a step in the right di-
rection."

The publication of *The Love Machine* should not be confused with a literary event. Not at all. There is nothing literary about Miss Susann—a former actress who became
somewhat successful in the fifties doing Schiffli embroidery

commercials with her poodle Josephine—or her writing. She is a natural storyteller, but her characters' motivations leave much to be desired and their mental processes are often just plain silly. I give you, herewith, a couple of typical sentences from *The Love Machine*, on what Miss Susann's heroines think while crying, an emotional act in which they indulge thirty-five times in the course of the novel (a figure that does not include the number of times they refrain from bursting into tears in order to prevent their mascara from running):

"She was sobbing for all the rejections, all the men she had loved for just one night, all the love she had never had."

And "She walked down to the river and knew the tears were running down her face. Oh God, it wasn't fair! It wasn't fair to put the heart and emotions of a beautiful woman into the heart of a peasant."

As for her dialogue ("My forte," says Miss Susann), I have never met anyone who talks quite the way the characters do in Miss Susann's books. On the other hand, I have never met any of Jacqueline Susann's friends, who apparently *do* talk that way. For example, James Aubrey, former president of CBS, who was convinced that he was the prototype for Robin Stone, called Miss Susann one day, and according to her, said, "Jackie, make me mean. Make me a son of a bitch." Like that.

But if Jacqueline Susann is no literary figure, she is nevertheless an extraordinary publishing phenomenon. Seven years ago, she gave up acting to write a rather charming little book about her poodle. It was called *Every Night, Josephine!*, it was published by Bernard Geis Associates, and it sold quite nicely. Then, in 1966, Geis published her first novel, *Valley of the Dolls*. The story of three young women who come to New York to find fame and fortune and end up hooked on pills, the book sold three hundred fifty thousand copies in hard cover and, far more astonishing, eight million copies in paperback. It is now among the top all-time best sellers and has just gone into its fifty-third Bantam softcover printing.

"When you think of all those guys out there with pipes and tweed suits who've been waiting years to write the great American novel," said Miss Susann's husband, "and you think how the one who's done it is little Jackie who never went to college and lives on Central Park South, well, it's really fabulous, isn't it?"

Yes.

As it happens, though, Mansfield's analysis of his wife's triumph is not quite accurate. Jacqueline Susann has not beaten out all those guys with pipes and tweeds, whoever they are. She has beaten out all those people who work in big cities, see the wages of sin thriving around them, read best-selling dirty novels, and say, "*I* can write that." In fact, they can not write that. And neither can all the sloppy imitators of Miss Susann's style—like Henry Sutton, Morton Cooper, and William Woodfolk, to name a few. Good *kitschy* writers are born, not made. And when Jacqueline Susann sits down at her typewriter on Central Park South, what spills out is first-rate *kitsch*.

What's more, it is sincere: unlike Sutton, who is slumming at the typewriter, Miss Susann believes every word she writes. And unlike Cooper and Woodfolk, whose novels are barely fictionalized, badly written accounts of celebrity lives, Miss Susann is—well, let her say it: "I am a thematic writer. In other words, I pick a theme and then the characters fall into place. With *Valley*, I never sat down and said, I'm going

to write about a prototype of Judy Garland or Ethel
Merman. I sat down and wondered, Why are we with the
pills and why are we with the funny farms today? The pills
became my theme." The theme of *The Love Machine* is that
power corrupts; the title refers not only to Robin Stone, who
becomes a machine as he gains power, but also to television
itself.

When *Valley of the Dolls* was published, it was not favor-
ably received by the critics. When it succeeded, most ob-
servers gave the credit to Mansfield and Miss Susann for
their frenetic promotional efforts. But a book that sells ten
million copies in all editions has more than just promotion
going for it. And *Valley* had a good deal more. For one thing,
it was the kind of book most of its readers (most of whom
were women and a large number of whom were teen-agers)
could not put down. I, for one, could not: I am an inveterate
reader of gossip columns and an occasional reader of movie
magazines, and, for me, reading *Valley of the Dolls* was like
reading a very, very long, absolutely delicious gossip column
full of nothing but blind items. The fact that the names were
changed and the characters disguised just made it more fun.

In addition, *Valley* had a theme with an absolutely mag-
netic appeal for women readers: it described the standard female fantasy—of going to the big city, striking it rich,
meeting fabulous men—and went on to show every reader
that she was far better off than the heroines in the book—
who took pills, killed themselves, and made general messes
of their lives. It was, essentially, a morality tale. And despite
its reputation, it was not really a dirty book. Most women, I
think, do not want to read hardcore pornography. They do
not even want to read anything terribly technical about the
sex act. What they want to read about is lust. And Jacqueline

Susann gave it to them—just as Grace Metalious did. Hot lust. Quivering lust. High-school lust. Sweaters are always being ripped open in Miss Susann's books. Pants are always being frantically unzipped. And everyone is always *wanting* everyone else. Take the women in *The Love Machine:*

- Ethel Evans, the promiscuous chubby from Hamtramck, who "wanted Robin so bad she physically ached."
- Maggie Stewart, newscaster-turned-actress: "She adored Adam. Then why did she always subconsciously think of Robin? Did she still want him? Yes, dammit, she did!"
- Judith Austin, face-lifted wife of the chairman of the board: "Oh God...she wanted him so! She needed someone to hold her and tell her she was lovely. She needed love. She wanted Robin!"

The Love Machine is a far better book than *Valley*—better written, better plotted, better structured. It is still, to be sure, not exactly a literary work. But in its own little subcategory of popularly written *romans à clef*, it shines, like a rhinestone in a trash can. The novel deals primarily with the rise and fall of Robin Stone, who rises and falls from the network presidency. His psychological problems are straight out of Hitchcock (to be specific, *Marnie*). And he runs through the lives of half a dozen women in the course of the book, leaving all of them scarred and mutilated—a couple of them literally so. With the possible exception of *Cosmopolitan* magazine, no one writes about masochism in modern women quite as horribly and accurately as Jacqueline Susann. Here, for example, is Amanda, the high-fashion model, speaking of her feelings for Robin Stone: "Sometimes I wish I didn't love him this much. Even after he's spent the night with me, when he leaves the following morning, I snuggle against the towel he's used. Sometimes I fold it up and put it in my tote bag and carry it with me all day. And I reach for that towel and touch it. And it almost smells of him . . . and I get weak." There is a streak of masochism in most women that should ensure Robin Stone's becoming one of the most popular characters in modern fiction.

The Love Machine is the second book in recent months based on the career of a television network president; the first, "The CanniBalS" by actor Keefe Braselle, was unreadable. Incidentally, Miss Susann sent the bound galleys of her book to her friend Aubrey a couple of months ago, but she has not heard a word in response. "I can't imagine why," she said. "Can you?"

Yes.

Simon and Schuster paid two hundred fifty thousand dollars for the hardcover rights of *The Love Machine*. (Miss Susann signed with them after buying out her contract with Bernard Geis for four hundred thousand dollars in an out-of-court settlement.) Bantam Books has advanced two hundred fifty thousand dollars for the paperback edition. A one-million-dollar movie offer from 20th Century-Fox has been turned down by the Mansfields, who think it is inadequate. An initial advertising budget of seventy-five thousand dollars is planned—much of it to pay for full-page newspaper spreads of Miss Susann's face, false eyelashes, and a one-shoulder silver sequined dress—and it is a fraction of what will ultimately be spent promoting the book. Said Simon and Schuster's Korda, "You have to push this book beyond regular book buyers to people who probably haven't been in a bookstore since *Valley of the Dolls* was published in hard cover."

In the meantime, Miss Susann has already begun her third novel. It is tentatively titled *The Big Man*. The theme, said Miss Susann, "is a girl's search for the big man. Her father was a big man. I think most girls have a thing for their fathers, don't you?"

Yes.

Eating and Sleeping With Arthur Frommer

June 1967

This year three hundred fifty thousand Americans—one out of five who travel to Europe—will go with Arthur Frommer. They will eat with Arthur Frommer and, as something of a witticism has it, sleep with Arthur Frommer.

Not content to leave it at that, some five thousand of them will write to Arthur Frommer. They will tell him they could never have done it without him; they will tell him they call his book the Bible; they will tell him they swear by him. Some will write ten-page, hand-written letters on lined paper telling Arthur Frommer every single hotel, restaurant, train, plane, bus, and beaded bag that happened to them on their way through Europe. Not a day passed, writes Mrs. Ray Westgate of Mattapoisett, Massachusetts, that she did not bless Arthur Frommer's name.

The Arthur Frommer involved is the author and publisher of *Europe on $5 a Day*, a 552-page guide to seventeen European cities, the best seller of the best-selling series of travel books published today. Begun as a modest 50-cent G.I. guide to European travel, it has become a $2.50 paperback written by Frommer and his wife, Hope, with yearly revisions and yearly sales of two hundred thousand copies.

It is the base of a travel-book empire that includes nine $5-a-Day books (Europe, Ireland, Spain, Greece, Israel, New York, Washington, South America, Mexico); six $5-and-$10-a-Day books (England, Scandinavia, Japan, Hawaii, the West Coast, the Caribbean); nine Dollar Wise guides providing cost information on travel for all price ranges; several miscellaneous books, including *Surprising Amsterdam* and *Happy Holland* by Frommer.

The empire also includes a quarterly newsletter, *The Wonderful World of Budget Travel*; the $5-a-Day Travel Club, which provides two $5-a-Day books, a copy of *Surprising Amsterdam* and travel discounts, all for $5 a year; and $5-a-Day Tours, a wholesale travel agency that this year will furnish thirty-five thousand American tourists with bed, breakfast, and guided tours in New York for $5 a you know what.

And coming soon: *America on $5 a Day*, a series of travel guides for senior citizens; *Europe on Five Diapers a Day*, the story of how Arthur and Hope travel with baby Pauline; and the biggest baby of all, the Arthur Frommer Hotels, the first of which will be under construction this summer in surprising Amsterdam.

The hotels, which Frommer describes as "less hotels than machines for sleeping," will provide no lobby, no convention facilities, no banquet halls, no sun lamps, no vibrators in the beds—nothing but a simple compartment with bed and sink for $3 a night per person. "I have a dream," says Arthur Frommer, "that one day in every city there will be a Conrad Hilton on one end of the scale and on the other an Arthur Frommer."

By the time that construction boom is over, the Bibles and blessings and swearings-by-Arthur-Frommer will probably have mounted to the point that there will be a small religious cult of Frommerites, recognizable—as they rush about saving nickels hither, dimes yon—by the simple aluminum $5 signs they will wear around their necks.

They are visible enough as it is. Today's Frommerite carries his big red book like a banner, daring natives to cheat him, challenging fellow tourists to underspend him. He worries as much about losing his book as he does his passport; and at least one anxiety dream has been reported: an employee of Paraphernalia claimed to have had a nightmare in which she was on a train going from France to Germany and could not find her Arthur Frommer.

The missionary behind all this is a black-haired, pink-faced, thirty-six-year-old lawyer who began the $5-a-Day books as a side interest eleven years ago. Frommer was raised in Jefferson City, Missouri, has a B.A. from NYU and a law degree from Yale, where he was a member of the Law Journal. During 1954–1955 he traveled widely and economically in Europe on his pay as a private first class in military intelligence in Germany. Before returning to New York and a job with the prestigious law firm of Paul, Weiss, Rifkind, Wharton and Garrison, he wrote and published a small pamphlet of travel tips for soldiers in Europe. Its immediate success convinced him there was a market for a book on budget travel.

In 1956 he went to Europe for a month's vacation to write the first *Europe on $5 a Day*, a 128-page book with a first printing of twenty thousand copies. By 1963 sales of that book and two others he had commissioned—New York and Mexico—and an increasing volume of mail forced him to give up his law practice.

Frommer is zealously devoted to his books. He has been known to telephone money-saving hints to his authors in the middle of the night. He refers to the hotels and restaurants recommended in his book as "my hotels" and "my restaurants." Once he turned red with rage on the Rue de Rivoli when one of his restaurants changed owners and raised its prices. Though he and Hope and baby Pauline live quite comfortably in a nine-room apartment on Central Park West, they rarely live according to their means abroad, and when they do, says Frommer, it is always a terrible mistake.

Frommer practices what Frommer preaches: the premise of all the $5-a-Day books is that budget travel is not a matter of necessity, it is a matter of choice. The only way. "Know the natives," shout Frommer and his band of writers. Live as they live on the level they live; eat breakfast in their kitchens; have croissants with their sanitation workers. And as you travel, actively disdain luxury travel, all its amenities, and, above all, the foolish tourists who travel that way, drink Coca-Cola, show pictures of their children to waiters, and meet only other foolish tourists who travel that way.

━━

This premise occasionally runs away with itself. Even in Washington, D.C., writes Beth Bryant in *Washington, D.C., on $5 a Day*, "it is far more delightful to stay in a grand, old reconverted townhouse . . . to share the TV lounge with FBI trainees, Supreme Court law clerks, and a female group of French social workers—than to spend $20 for a swank room in a 16th Street hotel where you meet no one but fellow American tourists." In fact, people who travel with $5-a-Day books have considerably less chance of meeting the natives than of meeting other people traveling with $5-a-Day books, all of them swearing by Arthur Frommer, saying they go to bed with him, and dying to compare costs to see who is saving more doing what.

Travel on $5 a day, a sum that includes room and board, can be accomplished by following Frommer's "rules of the game." Never, for example, take a room with a bath. Don't be put off by hotels without impressive façades and lobbies. Never patronize a restaurant without a menu in its window. Don't go to Washington while the cherry trees are in bloom, Israel during Passover, or Radio City Music Hall at night, when the rates go up. The cafeteria is king. And if the resulting trip bears some resemblance to the one Bean Blossom Township High School's graduating class took to New York in Lillian Ross's "The Yellow Bus," well, that's how it has to be in the wonderful world of budget travel. "My readers do not go for a gourmet experience," says Frommer.

My own experience, shared by many, is that budget travel is not a matter of choice, only of necessity. I like ice-cube machines in my hotel, gourmet experiences twice a day, please, and I have no desire whatsoever to sit in a TV lounge with an FBI trainee. But I have traveled with $5-a-Day books and find them utterly indispensable. Their bread-and-butter details—on public transportation, cultural events, hotels and restaurants—are unequaled, essential for all but the least cost-conscious travelers. More important, the books have convinced thousands of Americans who probably would never otherwise have traveled abroad that it is possible to do so on a severely limited budget.

They have also made it possible for several hundred of them to pursue a free-lance writing career of a sort. The $5-a-Day books now contain long sections of reader suggestions culled from reader mail and rewarded with a copy of a $5-a-Day book; many of them are useful; many are terrifyingly ingenious. "When we leave on our trip," writes Martin Jansson of Bowie, Maryland, "our suitcases are bulging with clothes, but many of them are garments to be worn just once more before discarding. This saves laundering, lightens the load progressively and gains space for purchases abroad. Our only problem resulting from this practice has been with cabin stewards, who . . . neatly pile the discarded clothes beside the berth. This necessitates a trip topside to throw them over the rail." The suggestions give the books a sort of tacky charm, something like Sidney Skolsky's column when just anyone was allowed to submit his Oscar picks.

If the books are indispensable, they are by no means perfect. The writing, with few exceptions, is humorless, uninteresting and given to rhetorical questions and exclamation points. ("What do the Dutch eat for lunch?" writes Frommer. "Well, most of them eat a second breakfast!") The books are also quite uneven, ranging from the excellent—Europe, England, Japan, Mexico, Greece, New York—to inadequate—South America, the Caribbean. Frommer emphatically denies the most frequent criticism of the books: that restaurants and hotels raise their prices as soon as they are mentioned. What happened more often, he says, is that they earn so much money as a result of being listed that they make improvements and become higher-quality establishments.

The books, particularly *Europe*, are remarkably up-to-date, an achievement Frommer credits to KLM, Royal Dutch Airways, which sponsors the book and receives in return its symbol on the book cover and a subsequent identification with budget travel. Unfortunately, Frommer has repaid KLM unwisely and too well: he fails to mention Icelandic Airlines, the only low-cost way to fly noncharter to Europe, and his enthusiasm for Amsterdam can only be looked upon with suspicion.

The surprising thing about surprising Amsterdam, it turns out, is that Frommer devotes more space to it than to any other European city. In addition, he insists that the city is the ideal gateway—arrival and departure point—for a European trip. Is it, as he claims, because the auto rentals are so low? Because of the sincere, warm way the Dutch speak English? Because of the taxfree shopping available at its airport? To use Frommer's style and punctuation: I doubt it!

These faults are regrettable in books that not only are otherwise incorruptible but also can easily afford to go unsubsidized, particularly by companies with such direct interest in the product. The food tasters for the *Guide Michelin* are not, after all, testing tire treads. One hopes Arthur Frommer will stop pinching his own pennies—by taking aid from KLM—so that others may better pinch theirs.

Publishing Prophets
for Profit

August 1968

There are those in the publishing world who say that the whole thing would have happened much sooner had it not been for *Life* magazine and its attack on poor Bridey Murphy in 1956. There are others—more disposed toward theories of occult causation—who believe that the spirit world just couldn't exert sufficient power over the publishing world until a few years ago. Still others—practical types—explain it as the book-buying public's response to the increasing complexity of modern living.

Whatever the reasons for it—and it remains for the sociologists to supply them—American publishers have discovered of late that there is a great deal of money to be made in convincing readers that the fault is not in themselves but in their stars. Books on parapsychology, mysticism, and the subjects that seem to follow inexorably from them—yoga, ESP, clairvoyance, precognition, telepathy, astrology, witches, mediums, ghosts, Atlantis, psychokinesis, prophecy, and, most of all, reincarnation—are flourishing. At least three paperback publishers—New American Library, Paperback Library, and Sherbourne Press—have begun series exclusively devoted to books on the occult; *Paperbound Books in Print* lists 203 titles under the category, "Parapsychology and the Supernatural." In hard cover, industry sources estimate that there are four times as many books on the subject now being printed as there were five years ago, though exact figures are virtually impossible to come by. The most recent parapsychological best seller, Jess Stearn's *The Search for the Girl with the Blue Eyes*, has sold forty-six thousand copies.

In these books, terms like "karma" and "odic force" appear, without any explanation or definition, as if they were in everyday use. The names of Jesus Christ, Benjamin Franklin, Abraham Lincoln, Arthur Conan Doyle, Keats, Yeats, Jung, Einstein, and Jackie Gleason (who once told Hedda Hopper that he was at times precognitive) are taken, sometimes in vain, as examples of famous men who were true believers. Respected writers who used to feel compelled to pretend skepticism when writing about the occult now confess to living with ghosts, speaking to dead relatives through mediums, and participating in automatic writing.

"The public interest has been way ahead of the publishers' response," said Lee Barker, executive editor of Doubleday and Company. "People in general want to read about these things. After all, there's the possibility of discovering the meaning of life. We can't get enough good books on the subject."

Doubleday, which published *The Search for Bridey Murphy* and *The Power of Prayer on Plants*, to name just two parapsychological classics, is probably the most active hard-cover publisher currently in this field. The fact that it cannot get enough good books on the subject has not prevented it, or other publishers, from printing what they think the market will bear. Books on parapsychology, Barker admits, are sadly inferior to most science fiction; indeed, they are also sadly inferior to most books written on gardening, pet care, and UFOs. It is almost incredible that so many authors could take such a fascinating subject and make it as boring as they do. Reading these books is a little like eating pressed duck: all the juice has been drained out of something that one knows was once meaty and succulent.

Generally speaking, there are two types of books written on parapsychology: those by psychics and those by journalists. The former, usually written with the assistance of a ghost writer (the term takes on new meaning here), are modest tables of how the author got his gift, how he resisted it for several years, and how he ultimately came to use it to help mankind without thought of personal profit. A recent example of the genre is *The Reluctant Prophet* (Doubleday), a book about a young man named Daniel Logan who became a big-time psychic as a result of his appearance on the David Susskind Show, where he predicted the 1967 summer riots, the end of the Northeast water shortage, and Elizabeth Taylor's 1966 Academy Award.

The second group, by far the more successful, are written by reporters/outsiders impressed by evidence they have uncovered or experienced themselves. What they have experienced, incidentally, has often been the result of contact with a stock company of psychical figures, which includes prophets Edgar Cayce and Jeane Dixon (who predicted President Kennedy's assassination), mediums Eileen Garrett and Arthur Ford (who figured in Bishop Pike's famous séance), and psychometrist Peter Hurkos. The most prominent authors in the outsider category are Ruth Montgomery and Jess Stearn. Miss Montgomery, the Hearst columnist who claimed to be without psychical talent when she wrote the 1965 best seller, *A Gift of Prophecy: The Phenomenal Jeane Dixon* (William Morrow and Company), now admits that she has been up to her neck in occult experiences for years and believes in reincarnation. Her forthcoming book, *Here and Hereafter* (Coward-McCann) is dedicated to her sister Margaret, with whom, Miss Montgomery writes, "I have trod many other happy paths in ages past."

Stearn, who is said to have lost his pot belly through yoga, is a former journalist whose early books were about various sexual persuasions and who moved into parapsychology about five years ago. Stearn's current book, *The Search for the Girl with the Blue Eyes* (Doubleday), is a second-rate Bridey Murphy adventure about an uninteresting small-town Canadian girl who turned out under hypnosis to be the reincarnation of another uninteresting small-town Canadian girl. Its publication has been advertised with a splash campaign in national magazines ("Left to right: Joanne MacIver, Susan Ganier, Jess Stearn" reads the caption under a picture of just two persons.) Its forty-six-thousand-copy sale would be respectable in any season, but it is small compared with Stearn's *Edgar Cayce—The Sleeping Prophet* (Doubleday), which sold 123,000 copies, spent thirty weeks on the best-seller list last year, and spawned a dozen paperback reprints and knockoffs on Cayce. (According to Stearn, the title *The Sleeping Prophet* came directly from Cayce, who communicated it from the spirit world to a New York medium named Bathsheba Asko-with.)

Among the Cayce books now on the stands are several by Cayce's son, Hugh Lynn, the director of the Association for Research and Enlightenment (ARE), a Virginia Beach, Virginia, organization devoted to carrying on the work of Edgar Cayce. This is not an altogether easy task, since Cayce has been dead for twenty-three years and no one with his astonishing psychical gifts has come forth to replace him. Nevertheless, the ARE bobbles along on waves of interest in Cayce (one being the result of a chapter in *Bridey Murphy*), and this very week is offering a seven-day program of study of Reincarnation and Karma, featuring a lecture on Presenting Reincarnation to Children, for twenty-six dollars, including meals.

Edgar Cayce, parapsychology's sleeping prophet, was born near Hopkinsville, Kentucky, in 1877. An unassuming man, Cayce (pronounced KAY-see) reached only the fifth grade of school at the age of fifteen, when he dropped out. He was humble, devout, and thoroughly mystified by the powers he began to display in his twenties, when it became clear that he could, in trance, diagnose the illnesses of patients he had never met, prescribe cures involving drugs he had never heard of, and use anatomical expressions he could not pronounce in a non-trance state. During his life, Cayce eked out a living as a photographer and supplemented his income with the modest sums he got for his diagnoses. He died in 1945.

Cayce's cures, now bound in a little black book and available for twenty-five dollars from the ARE, are a strange combination of medicine, folk medicine, and osteopathy, delivered in a convoluted, almost incomprehensible style of speech. (This, for example, is Edgar Cayce supposedly predicting the Great Depression: "Better that a few points were missed here and there, even in a spectacular rise or fall, than to be worrying where the end would be. Forget not the warning here.") Cayce's record as a diagnostician is well documented: his secretary made three copies of each reading he gave, and many of the people who wrote him for help are alive to tell the tale.

One such witness is William Sloane, an eminent editor who probably did more to bring parapsychology into respectable publishing houses than any other man. Sloane was the first man in the book trade to publish the work of Dr. J. B. Rhine, the grand old man of telepathy and director of the Duke University Institute for Parapsychology; he bought the first book written on Edgar Cayce (*There Is a River* by Thomas Sugrue), commissioned the second (*Many Mansions* by Gina Cerminara), and paid the first advance to a Denver amateur hypnotist named Morey Bernstein for the story of his experience regressing a Denver housewife back to a previous life as an Irish homebody named Bridey Murphy. Sloane, himself something of a sensitive, once called five cards in a row correctly off the top of a shuffled deck in order to convince his salesmen there was something to telepathy.

In 1940 Thomas Sugrue, a writer who felt he owed his life to a Cayce reading, sent the manuscript of *There Is a River* to Sloane, then at Holt, Rinehart and Winston. "I read it," said Sloane, at present director of the Rutgers University Press. "Now there isn't any way to test a manuscript like this. So I did the only thing I could do. A member of my family, one of my children, had been in great and continuing pain. We'd been to all the doctors and dentists in the area and all the tests were negative and the pain was still there. I wrote, told him my child was in pain and would be at a certain place at such-and-such a time, and enclosed a check for twenty-five dollars. He wrote back that there was an infection in the jaw behind a particular tooth. So I took the child to the dentist and told him to pull the tooth. The dentist refused—he said his professional ethics prevented him from pulling sound teeth. Finally, I told him he would have to pull it. One tooth more or less didn't matter, I said—I couldn't live with the child in such pain. So he pulled the tooth and the infection was there and the pain went away. I was a little shook. I'm the kind of man who believes in X rays. About this time, a member of my staff who thought I was nuts to get involved with this took even more precautions in writing to Cayce than I did, and he sent her back facts about her own body only she could have known. So I published Sugrue's book."

There Is a River is probably the best of the Cayce books. Unlike Stearn's book, it has the virtue of the chronological order. But almost every book on Cayce is limited by the prophet's awkward expression and by the nonmedical readings he gave. Edgar Cayce's adventures into reincarnation—known as his "life readings"—are so foolish as to make his medical record very nearly suspect. One may be very partial to modest stories about Alabama housewives who lie down on couches and regress to become Scottish minstrels, but it is hard to cope with Cayce's panoramic regressions. In his life readings, almost everyone he ever read for turned out to have existed in previous lives with everyone else he ever read for—on the same Crusades, in the same wilderness, together in Jerusalem, together on the lost continent of Atlantis. Cayce, his wife, and his secretary had been together, marching through Georgia, Cairo, and Rome, in at least ten different incarnations. Cayce's son, Hugh Lynn, once came to his father for a life reading after breaking off an unhappy engagement, only to be given the reassuring information that he was well rid of the girl since he'd been married to her in three previous lifetimes and she'd been rotten to him in all three of them. This suggests that Edgar Cayce may at times have been a better father than a seer.

The Search for Bridey Murphy, published in 1956, was written by Morey Bernstein under the influence of Cayce's life readings. Bernstein had not only read There Is a River and Many Mansions but also did some research on his book at the ARE. Bridey Murphy—which Doubleday bought from William Sloane, who felt the evidence in the manuscript did not stand up—sold 150,000 copies in six weeks; then a Life magazine story offering a nonspiritual explanation for Bridey's "reincarnation" stopped its sale dead. (It is a charming book, recently reissued in paperback by Lancer Books with an extra chapter debunking the Life story.) Lee Barker at Doubleday thinks the exposé probably was the cause for postponing, for a few years at least, the surge in parapsychological literature. Not until Ruth Montgomery's book on Jeane Dixon, nine years later, did the field have another big best seller.

There does seem to be something to parapsychology. (This, along with its appeal to people unwilling to look within themselves for the source of their difficulties, probably accounts for the popularity of these books.) The work done at Duke University has shown that telepathy and clairvoyance can be scientifically documented. How they work and what they mean are still unclear; like the Rosetta stone before

Champollion, they remain a tantalizing puzzle promising a great deal, perhaps a great deal more than they ultimately deliver. As for reincarnation, there is little evidence that it exists—a fact that does not alter one whit its attractions for any man who has made a mess of his current life on earth.

This much *is* clear: most of humanity muddles through without relying on parapsychology. We use the telephone, not telepathy. In fact, some publishers—a quiet few—have begun to wonder whether there is not some danger in exposing readers to the view of events that parapsychology represents. It may be that these books—particularly the sketchy, overstated, hastily put-together items that dominate the field—make it difficult for the susceptible to deal with their lives. As publisher William Sloane put it, "When a man is drowning, it may be better for him to try to swim than to thrash around waiting for divine intervention."

The Diary of a
Beach Wife

This article is the closest thing to fiction I have ever written. I was never a beach wife. I do not have children. The Jewish writers I know have straight hair. We do summer in East Hampton, though, and we do know a lot of beach wives. I promise you I will never become one.

May 1969

July 2

Here we are. In Springs, the artists' colony of East Hampton, Long Island, only two and a half hours from New York on the Long Island Expressway—if you happen to be driving at three in the morning and no other cars are on the highway. Came out yesterday, in a rented station wagon, with one mother's helper (Scarsdale High School, uses Clearasil) and the kids (who demanded twelve gas-station stops and threw fried clams all over the Howard Johnson's in Riverhead). All in all, the trip took five and one-half hours. Not that I have any right to complain about the distance: it was *my* idea that we rent a house here. In the Hamptons. A clutch of charming little towns at the Eastern tip of Long Island, with giant old beach houses, glossy white beaches, fresh-caught lobsters, acres of potato fields, and a summer population consisting of just Everyone. Westhampton, containing just Everyone in advertising. Quogue, containing just Everyone on Wall Street. Southampton, containing just Everyone in society. East Hampton, containing just Everyone in the arts. As for Springs, it's on the Bay, and is, I must confess, a woodsy and not entirely chic appendage to East Hampton. No town of its own to speak of, but Main Street, East Hampton is ten minutes away—two long blocks of one-story white shops straight out of Olde New England, and no bathing suits and bare feet allowed. Keeps the real-estate prices up and the riffraff out.

In Springs, the mosquitoes bloom earlier, the sun heats hotter, and the wood ticks are saucier than in East Hampton proper. But it's what we could afford—thirty-five hundred dollars for the short season (July 1–Labor Day), and, as the rental agent said back on that snowy day in February when we signed the lease, the house is across the street from the cemetery where Jackson Pollock is buried, just down the block from critic Harold Rosenberg, and right next door to Willem de Kooning. I can see the headlines now: "EXPRESSIONIST PAINTER SUCCUMBS TO

MANHATTAN HOUSEWIFE: 'It Must Have Been My Bill Blass Bathing Suit That Got Him,' Says Temptress."

Frank is commuting Thursday nights for long weekends. It's not ideal, but what can you do? It's either this or sweating it out in the city. Adam and Amanda will be brown and healthy. The mother's helper's skin will clear up. I will grow dill and tomatoes and do all the things I've been meaning to do since Wellesley: search my soul, read Jane Austen, and stalk the wild asparagus. Ellie Trillin will also be out here (her house is two doors from a cottage rented by Sherman Rogin, the Jewish novelist who shot his first wife in the ankle), and we've vowed to take exercise classes at Kounovsky's in Westhampton. Frank promises he'll take two weeks off in July and spend them out here. "VACATIONING GOTHAM LAWYER SLASHES NUDE PAINTING OF WIFE BY FAMOUS ARTIST." All in all, it shouldn't be too bad. A little separation is good for any couple, right? And everybody does it. Year after year. People wouldn't keep doing it over and over again if it was bad, would they? Or would they?

Before I left, I bumped into Jill Corman. A skinny bohemian one class ahead of me who kept a bottle of May wine under the bathtub. I told her I was doing the Beach Wife thing for the summer. "You must be crazy," she said, "Leaving your husband alone in the city with all those secretaries." Told her there was no other way. Said the summer air in New York wasn't fit to breathe. Mumbled something about the possibility of rioting in the streets this summer. "But what about all those predatory females in town?" she said. "What about all those single painters and/or writers at the beach?" said I. I thought I handled her very nicely. But I keep wondering. What if she is right?

July 7

July Fourth weekend glorious. Four days of perfect weather. Everyone says it won't last. Everyone refers in Ominous Tones to the summer of 1967, when it rained all of August and even the tomatoes hated it. I refuse to listen to them. Frank left this morning on the 6:13 for New York and said he would be back Friday. "I thought you said you'd be out Thursday," I said. "I'll try," he said. The house has bats. I'm going into town to see a man about an extermination. Then, off to the East Hampton Coast Guard Beach, where (according to yesterday's *New York Times Book Review*) the literati hang out. Saul Bellow. Sherman Rogin. Barney Rosset, publisher of Grove Press. Norman Mailer, here to make a film. "ANGRY YOUNG NOVELIST TO STAR WELLESLEY GRAD ('58) IN CINEMA VÉRITÉ FILM."

July 14

My first whole week: Monday recovered from weekend. Tuesday spent in East Hampton laundromat. Wednesday gardened. Thursday cleaned house. Friday prepared for arrival of husband and houseguests. Washed hair. Cleaned nails. Shaved legs. Oiled body. Ate celery for lunch. Spent $75 at supermarket and $50 at liquor store. Took children to station to meet The Daddy Train. Mine wore flannel pajamas. Everyone else's wore Pucci pajamas.

Frank arrived. Complained about Long Island Rail Road. Said air conditioning in parlor car didn't work. Griped about life in town: he eats TV dinners at night and is growing a mold in a dirty coffee cup. Houseguests arrived in time for dinner and polished off twelve ears of corn, two loaves French bread, and one grilled striped bass prepared according to Craig Claiborne's recipe in last week's *Times*. After dinner, houseguests sighed and said they always sleep better in the country and they always eat more in the country. Translation: they are going to sleep all day and eat all of my food. The weekend: I rushed from supermarket to stove to sink to beach to supermarket to stove to sink. Seven meals and four bottles of rum later, houseguests departed, promising to send present which will not begin to reward me for the time, effort, and money I spent on them. Today it is Monday, and I am recovering from the weekend. Like that. Meanwhile, I have polished off twelve Agatha Christies and three Rex Stouts. I'm saving Jane Austen for the long nights of August.

July 17

Life here is not quite what I expected. For one thing, Willem de Kooning does not live next door. His ex-wife lives next door. And Harold Rosenberg rented his house down the block to a certified public accountant and is off in Crete for the summer. As for Jackson Pollock, he is definitely buried across the street, though I haven't been able to find his grave.

The East Hampton Coast Guard Beach is beautiful—clean, white rolling dunes that seem to stretch for miles into the blue sea, quiet and private, houses as big as hotels fronting on it, all of them covered with climbing roses. On Sundays there's a show-biz strip (where I overheard Lauren Bacall tell Adolph Green she uses Noskote to keep her nose from burning), a clutch of psychiatrists (who all play crib-bage), and there's even a homosexual belt. But you would hardly know there was anything literary about it. I did spot Sherman Rogin walking his dog down the beach yesterday. He is adorable—great soulful brown eyes and curly black hair that looks like clusters of black grapes. I think he winked at me.

But otherwise, during the week, I see only women and their children and their mother's helpers and their styro-foam containers holding sandwiches and Vienna wafers and plums and soft drinks. Thus far, I have sat with the Mommies, the Huntresses, and the Climbers. The Mommies all wear wretched, wrinkled one-piece bathing suits and ex-press concern over violence in fairy tales, the price of chuck at the Bohack, and the difficulty of boycotting grapes during months when it is necessary to pack lunches daily. Much talk of Sally and Portia and what horrid children they are. Or what horrid mothers they are. I forget which. The Huntresses are three psychoanalysts' wives who drink Bloody Marys and discuss divorce all day long. One of them—who is aptly named Diana—has already broken off with her husband. She bought a new bathing suit at Jax in Southampton and wanders up and down the beach with scarves trailing, searching for a new man. Last week she and a girl friend went to L'Oursin, the discothèque-barge, but all they emerged with were headaches from the strobe lights and a joint of marijuana a pitying eighteen-year-old boy slipped them. Diana is undaunted and has her eye on an apparently single creature who looks like a Czech film maker and smokes Gauloises. No one knows who he is.

The Climbers are all married to Wall Street types, wear matching bathing-suit-and-jacket ensembles, and spend the day discussing how they can meet all the celebrities in the area. Their usual ploy is to introduce their children to the children of celebrities in hopes of meeting their parents. "Do you know who that is?" one of them said to me, pointing to a three-year-old child who was busy eating sand. "No," I said. "That is Sean McCourt," she explained, "the Broadway playwright's wife's son by her second marriage." "Oh," I said. The Climbers spend two days a week in Southampton—one having their hair done at Lupe's, the other exercising at a private club. All of them have calluses on their hands from working out on trapezes—a brutal fact that Ellie and I discovered and thereupon canceled plans for Kounovsky's.

Adam and Amanda love the beach, partly because they are allowed to go to the bathroom in the ocean owing to the lack of facilities. Amanda, who managed to build a twig house out of poison ivy, has made friends with Julie Henry, the daughter of Harry Henry, the Broadway producer. "HARRY HENRY BUYS N.Y. MATRON'S NOVEL FOR MUSICAL: 'All I Have to Do Now Is Write the Book,' Says Housewife."

July 24

Sherman Rogin on the beach again. This time I'm positive he winked at me. And I could swear he deliberately walked his dog past me several times just to sneak extra looks at my Rudi Gernreich black bikini with plastic inserts. Ellie says he is having an affair with Rustine Pepper, the wife of the *Village Voice* columnist, in whose driveway his dog was seen recently tethered. What's more, she says that the dog, a German shepherd, is definitely the prototype of the Doberman pinscher which developed such fascinating fetishistic tastes in his last novel. "JEWISH NOVELIST BREAKS UP LAWYER'S MARRIAGE. Guard Dog Keeps Angry Husband Away from East Hampton Lovenest."

July 29

Our first rainy weekend. Frank arrived Thursday for his first three-day weekend since the Fourth, expecting to find cheerful babies and a tanned and terrific me. We sat in the house with wet sheets and mildewed air. Kids screamed all day. We stared Ingmar Bergman–like at each other all night. There was a movie playing in town but we had seen it in the city in April. There was a movie at the Bridgehampton Drive-In, but it starred Doris Day. Sunday, in desperation, we went relentlessly antiquing. Ended up at Ballasses in Amagansett and bought three thoroughly mysterious objects good only for trailing plants over. Frank left this morning, cursing me, the Long Island Rail Road, and his brand-new bathing suit, and blaming all of us for the weather. It makes sense. He's a rational man. He knows there's no use blaming God.

August 4

A party at Hank Henry's. I met his wife—on the Coast
Guard beach, where else?—and she invited us. Unbelievable
house—eight thousand dollars for the summer, one second
from the beach, and four in help, including a waiter who
served drinks with a toothpick in his mouth. Everyone who
was anyone was there, my dear. Fags. Lesbians, Lyricists.
Composers. Actresses. Playwrights. Authors. What we were
doing on the list I don't know—I think we were being used
in about the same way a florist uses green leaves to fill out a
vase of roses. I was so nervous about going that I spent a fortune on a long chiffon culotte outfit that was absolutely
transparent and made me look as if I had nothing on underneath. Frank thought it was obscene, but Sherman Rogin
loved it. I told him how much I admired his work. He told
me how much he admired my ensemble. A wonderful
evening. Though, now that I think of it, there wasn't really
much reason to have been worried about it: the conversation dwelled mainly on the price of real estate in the area.
Today is the mother's helper's day off. I'm taking the kids to
the game preserve. Afterward, I think we'll go to the bakery
in Southampton—which just happens to be next door to
the bookstore where I can buy the collected works of S.
Rogin.

August 6

A night with the ladies. Incredible. For one thing, lots of
drinking. I felt so old—I always associated drinking-with-

the-girls with the ladies tippling martinis at Schrafft's. For another thing, the conversation: they talked of nothing but which beach wives were being unfaithful, with whom, and how. It seems that the Czech film maker has turned out to be an advertising illustrator and has taken up with a blonde surgeon's wife from Passaic who is out for the summer while her unsuspecting husband does open-heart surgery all week at Downstate Medical. Meanwhile, the word from Bridgehampton is that a television newscaster and his wife have switched mates with a couple of anthropologists across the street and are living happily ever after. Everyone searched her mind for more stories of infidelity that led to happy endings. No one could think of any. All that I could think of were the tales of indiscretion I used to hear during my summers in the city—like the one about the Random House editor seen necking on the grass in Central Park with a copy reader—but no one seemed to want to hear tales about what might be going on in town. I suppose no one wants to think about it. I know I don't. The ladies insist there is as much hanky-panky out here as there is in the city. Ellie says it isn't so. Not that she would have any idea: the high point of her summer was the night a peacock escaped from a private game collection and spent the night honking and defecating on her patio. I was so depressed by the evening and all the girl talk that I called Frank when I got home. He was out. "LAWYER ARRESTED IN EAST SIDE ORGY: Claims He Was Driven to It After Five Weeks as Summer Bachelor." All the ladies agree that if their husbands were unfaithful to them, they would know. I wonder.

August 11

It rained again all weekend. Frank has taken to muttering something about how he is paying $100-a-minute for a vacation in the rain. Adam and Amanda both have summer colds, with little red noses on their little red faces. Worms have struck the tomatoes and a rabbit ate the dill. I am fighting back with chicken wire and insecticide.

August 12

This is not my week. Today the doorbell rang, and standing there was a fresh-faced seventeen-year-old girl. "I hear there's somebody young living here," she said. I went to get the mother's helper. And all my illusions about how I still manage to look seventeen vanished.

August 18

Sherman Rogin called this morning and asked if I'd like to have dinner with him. Tonight. I know I shouldn't have accepted, but I couldn't help it. Frank has been postponing the two weeks he was supposed to spend out here—to the point that I'll be lucky if he gets out for a four-day Labor Day weekend. And in the meantime, it's hard not to feel that my weekdays are spent in a world of ladies and little people. It's the Indian reservation, with all the men off making war and wampum and all the ladies sitting home drying ears of corn.

Of course, after Sherman called, I felt so dreadful about accepting I decided to call him back and tell him I couldn't possibly go through with it. I couldn't reach him. I thought of Frank, calling me every night, not going to see the new Steve McQueen movie because he knew I would want to see it when I got back to town, making last weekend so nice by deigning to play tennis with me and taking me to Gordon's for crispy duck and chocolate cake. I called him in town, all weepy and ready to make some muddled confession. When I got through to him, he was so annoyed at being interrupted in the middle of a meeting that I determined to go through with the date after all. "LAWYER'S WIFE ARRESTED FOR BITING AUTHOR ON HEAD: 'I Couldn't Help It,' She Said Later. It Looked Like Black Grapes.'" Actually, I doubt that anything will happen. We're just having dinner. You can have dinner with a man if you're married and have it not mean anything at all. He's probably just blocked on his new novel and wants to talk to a sympathetic soul. And if, in the course of the evening, he happens to attack and rape me— well, we're civilized people. I could hardly yell for the police. I'd just have to submit.

August 19

Well. He picked me up at 7:30. I had spent two hours figuring out what to wear. I couldn't very well appear in my diaphanous culottes. So I wore a little white skirt and a little red shirt and I looked just like the Peck & Peck girl I am. We drove to Montauk, to a fish place overlooking the water. And there I was, sitting with a glamorous, sensual, potentially violent novelist, who spent most of the evening talking about his mother and whether he should trade in his car for a Fiat and where you can buy the best clams in the area. Then we went for a drink at a bar in East Hampton and talked some more. About my mother's helper and her prospects for higher education. About Adam's day camp. About the prices at the Farmer's Market in Amagansett. And nothing happened. That's right. I didn't know whether to be elated or disappointed. I think he expected me to be whatever he thought a lady in a transparent dress would be, and I thought he would be some kind of romantic madcap. I don't know. In any case, he dropped me off at 11:30 and *chucked me under the chin*. Like I was his kid sister. There I was, home before midnight, feeling completely foolish and horribly guilty. As well I might have. Under the right circumstances—whatever the right circumstances might have been—I might have let that man have his way with me. I might have become pregnant by him. And produced a child that was clearly not my husband's. "PATERNITY SUIT INTRODUCES GENETIC LAW: Blue-Eyed Lawyer Accuses Blue-Eyed Wife of Going Elsewhere for Brown-Eyed Child." Frank is coming out today on the 5:34, and I'm probably overdoing things, but I'm planning to bring martinis to the train. If he smoked a pipe or wore slippers, I'd bring them too. And I've promised myself to ask him all about his cases. And cook lobsters, even though I hate dropping the poor things into boiling water. Monday I begin Jane Austen.

September 9

We're back in New York. I almost cried as we drove across the Triborough Bridge. I'm so happy to be back. If I never have to clean another grain of sand out of a car, or remove tar from my kids' feet with turpentine, or set foot in the town of East Hampton again, I'll be absolutely overjoyed. Last week I told Frank I'd like to go to Europe next summer. He nodded. "What are we going to do with the kids?" he said. "Leave them with your mother," I said. He said he would think about it. And then, before my eyes, he picked up the real-estate section and began scanning Houses for Sale—Long Island. Hmmmmm. "LAWYER'S WIFE BECOMES L.I. HOSTESS WITH MOSTEST: East Hampton Home Becomes Salon for Summering Artists and Writers." Hmmmmm. Well, I suppose there are worse fates.

An Interview With
Mike Nichols

The most dangerous thing for a journalist writing a profile is to worry more about what the person he is writing about will think of his article than what the people he is writing for will think. That happens to be the position in which I found myself when writing about Mike Nichols, and it made me vow never again to write anything about him, or about anyone I particularly care for. Everyone I know who has interviewed Nichols has had this experience: he is smart and kind and funny and he listens and he ultimately makes me sound like a blathering fool when describing him. So I will stop.

December 1968

Q: First of all, I understand you've been in New York for three straight weeks, and I wondered how it happened that you were in one place for that long a time.

NICHOLS: Well, I didn't go anywhere. We start shooting *Catch-22* next month, and the producer and Buck Henry (the screenwriter) and some of the people on the picture came here, because I didn't want to go to California, and they indulged me.

Q: When I interviewed you about Buck Henry, you told me someone once asked you about California and you said you had found peace in Hollywood.

NICHOLS: That was a joke. Buck asked me that—that's how we met. He said, "Do you like it here?" And I said, "Yes. Here under the shadow of this great big tree, I have found peace." It was at a party at Jane Fonda's house and was, in fact, in the shadow of a great tree.

Q: Do you find Hollywood not conducive to working?

NICHOLS: Living, I would say.

Q: Most people say it's easier to live there.

NICHOLS: Well, yes it is. But who says that's good?

Q: I wanted to ask about *Catch-22*, because I just saw Joseph Heller's *We Bombed in New Haven*, which has more or less the same theme, and it seemed a little old-fashioned and World War Twoish. I wondered if you thought *Catch-22* was still timely?

NICHOLS: I don't think of it as, one, being about World War Two and two—perhaps I'd better change that to (a) being about World War Two and (b) timely or not timely. I think of it as a picture about dying and a picture about when you get off. It's a picture about choosing at what point you take control over your life and say, "No, I won't. *I* decide. *I* draw the line." And also, "timely" is, I think, a dangerous word. You know, is *Grand Illusion* timely? It's just a great picture.

Q: You once said you were laid out for years. What are your plans after you finish *Catch-22*?

NICHOLS: I have an obligation to do two more pictures, but they can be whenever and whatever I want. I think I have found a play I want to do with Elaine May after *Catch-22*. There were three of us in Chicago—Elaine, Paul Sills, and me—and we started a theater together and then started the group called Compass that became Second City and we're now talking about starting a theater again together in New York, to close the circle and get back to what we did. In that course of planning what we wanted to do, we found a French play that seems to me about what Elaine's and my work has been about, and it seemed necessary for us to play it.

Q: Are you going to act in it?

NICHOLS: Yes. I hope. It's very dangerous to talk about something that far away because *Catch-22* will probably take most of my life.

Q: Did you ever expect *The Graduate* to become what it has?

NICHOLS: No, of course not. It never crossed any of our minds.

Q: Was there a point when you began to think that it might happen? Was there one night?

NICHOLS: There was a night that we previewed it in New York, at the RKO 86th or the Loew's 81st or the Loew's 86th—anyway, a huge theater on the East Side that holds like twenty-six hundred or three thousand people. We were showing our work print, with all the splices in it. And I had a box in my lap, running the sound, because we hadn't dubbed it yet. The theater was packed, and I spent—naturally, as I always do—I spent all my time saying to everybody around me, "Is it too dark? Is it too light? Is it too loud? Should I make it louder? Can you hear it? It's too loud now, isn't it?" and after a while, I stopped, because what the audience was doing was really rather shocking. It sort of sounded like a prize fight. I have never heard an audience make that noise before. Laugh like that. Shout like that. Yell like that. And for the last five minutes of the picture they began to cheer and they didn't stop. And I was very taken aback, and in my own bizarre way, pleased. And then I ran the hell out of the theater.

Q: What did you do then?

NICHOLS: I went home and got mad at myself that I hadn't stayed.

Q: When I saw *The Graduate*, I felt that it was totally about my life. It was such a California movie, and my adolescence there came rushing back at me.

NICHOLS: Well, have you ever had the experience of seeing something the details of which really had nothing to do with your life and yet you sit there and can say, "That's my life"?

I'm not saying that that's a quality that *The Graduate* had, because how do I know? But it happens with films and it happens with people. I mean, I can see *L'Avventura* or *8 1/2* and say, "That's my life." It has nothing to do with the details of my life.

Q: And one film has nothing to do with the other.

NICHOLS: That's right. In fact, they're almost opposite extremes. But that experience is possible. Somebody gets his own life on the nose, he really gets it the way it was for him, and we can sit there and say, "Yes, I remember that."

Q: Once, when speaking about *The Graduate*, you said that when you were making it you didn't think you were making a film about a generation but about a young man of a certain age. "We were that age once," you said. "People forget that." I thought that was interesting because it seemed to indicate you didn't think too much of this thing called the generation gap.

NICHOLS: Well, it seems to me a mistake to generalize people. They've been generalized so much—"the middle class," "the kids"—that a very odd thing has happened: they actually think of themselves as instances of a generality. Which I don't think is a possible way to live. I think that there are gaps between people. But I find often as large a gap between me and somebody my own age as I do between myself and somebody nineteen, or fifteen, or, in the case of my daughter, five. But as soon as you generalize it, I think you lose particulars. Yes, sure, something is happening. But it's been generalized so much and made into slogans so much that to undo the kind of magazine-propaganda aspect of phrases like "generation gap," it's best to get specific and talk about things between individuals.

Q: I'd like to see *The Graduate* again.

NICHOLS: Me, too. I haven't seen it since it opened.

Q: You should—although every time I see a movie six months after it's opened, the film is cracking and the sound is bleeping.

NICHOLS: That's why I don't go. Because it's so painful. Opening night of *Virginia Woolf*—that is, the first press night—Mr. Warner in his wisdom decided the whole world press was to see it all together on one night. And they all did, in fact, see it together on one night. And when they changed from the first reel to the second reel, the screen went black—not gray, not very dark, but *black*. And I went, in my calm way, and screamed at the manager. And he put his arms around my shoulders and said, "Mike, baby, don't worry. We've got the best projectionist in the business up there." And I had to comfort myself with the fact that he was the best projectionist in the business, although the screen was totally black. I can't go to see my pictures in a theater because they're always too light or too dark or you can't hear them. I make such a pest of myself that the people in the theaters dread seeing me come. So I just stay away.

Q: Have you done that? Arrived at the projection booth and said, "Listen . . ."?

NICHOLS: I used to do that with *Virginia Woolf*. And they began to think of me as some kind of crank, you know, that they had to suffer, that had these illusions that the audience should hear the dialogue and possibly even see the film. I finally decided that I was driving myself and them crazy, and I stayed away. It doesn't seem to bother most people. I once went to see *Torn Curtain* and you couldn't hear it and you couldn't see it. But the audience didn't seem to mind. They sat there very happily, laughing occasionally—I don't know at what, because you couldn't hear the dialogue. The cutter on *The Graduate*, Sam O'Steen, went to see it at a theater in Los Angeles, and it wasn't out of focus—it looked like a psychedelic light show. There were vague, vague human shapes playing across the screen. And he went running to the projection booth—in which the projectionist was screwing on the floor with an usherette. So at that point you have to say to yourself, Life is more important than art.

Q: This is a naïve question, but film is a very mysterious thing to me, and I don't understand how you just went out there and made a movie. How did you find out about all those mysterious sound devices and mysterious words like "looping"?

NICHOLS: I just held my nose and jumped in.

Q: But did you feel like an imbecile?

NICHOLS: I still do.

Q: You do?

NICHOLS: Oh, of course. All the time. Don't you?

Q: Oh no, because I'm not doing anything terribly hard. It's just me and a typewriter. It's not me and a million technicians and budgets and deadlines.

NICHOLS: Well, I'll tell you two stories. One is about the first day of shooting on *Virginia Woolf*. The scene was Richard and Elizabeth coming through the front door, going to the living room and turning on the light. And her saying, "Jesus H. Christ," or whatever she said. And it was not only my first day on the picture, it was my first day on a movie set. I had thought and thought about it and had drawn little pictures and made little plans, and Richard and Elizabeth were all made up and ready to go and there were a hundred and fifty men standing around with their arms folded, and I suddenly thought, How do I get them through the door? If the camera is facing the door, won't the door hit the camera when it opens? And if it's far back enough, won't they walk into the camera when they come in?

Q: But you knew cameras moved, right?

NICHOLS: Well, I did know that. But didn't know where to put it because I wanted to see them close. And then I thought, If it's too close, the door will hit it. Well, everybody had all sorts of suggestions. I mean, it was clear that I was in naked panic. And I had special advisers. And finally the cameraman said, "See, we'll do this and they'll come in and we'll move and we'll pan them and they'll disappear momentarily behind the wall as they walk toward the kitchen and we'll see them reappear again and it will be very interesting." And I said, "Well, what's it for?" He said, "Well, it's interesting." And I thought, Oh, Christ. Now I have to do this very hard thing. They know more than I do, but I have to decide what it's going to be because I know what I am going to tell and they don't. That was a terrible minute. And I just said, All right. Pull yourself together and do it. And I did. And then, you begin to learn it. You begin to discover what it is. There are various sorts of mysteries that are cleared up by accident. The cameramen are always saying—and this is absolutely their domain—they are always saying, "Two-eight." Or, "Three-five." Or, "Four-eight." And I would think, Well, they know why they want it at two-eight. It's not my business. We've talked about the mood of the scene and how I want it to look. Weeks and weeks of the cameraman's saying "two-eight" and "three-five" had gone by. One day, I happened to be looking through the camera at a stand-in, and he said, "Two-eight." Then he said, "Change it to three-five." And as I looked, it got brighter. "You mean that's it?" I said. "That's all it is? It's just a diaphragm that opens up or closes down?" He said, "Of course, you ass. What did you think it was?" And you begin to discover that most of the technical things are rather like that—they can be explained, they can be understood, and they can be dealt with. The big decision, the hard decision, is how to use them. To understand them is not that rough. You know what it's like? Do you remember in kindergarten when you had subjects like shoelace tying?

Q: Yes. Only we had apple cutting.

NICHOLS: We had French. When I was five I couldn't tie my shoelaces yet, but they started teaching us French from playing cards. We never cut apples. We did tie shoelaces. And it's very much like that thing where you think, I'll never tie this shoelace; I don't understand. And then after a while you are tying it and then you forget about it and then you know how to tie a shoelace.

Q: There was a long piece in *The New Yorker* on *The Graduate* which I had a little trouble reading. . . .

NICHOLS: I couldn't finish it, I have to admit.

Q: Well, in the end, the writer said of you that you had thus far attempted nothing that strained at the limits of your talent.

NICHOLS: Well, I think that's a difficult thing to know about someone else. As far as he knows—what if I have exceeded the limits of my talent and there is nothing more I can do? It's very hard to know that about someone else. As to the article, the writer was more interested in the picture than I am. He wrote so long—I have never seen such a long piece on a movie.

Q: The other night I met a man who told me he was writing a book on how to write movie criticism and how to judge a movie. And I thought, Oh, God, no. I find it horrifying that people take these things so seriously.

NICHOLS: I couldn't agree more. It's like writing a book on how to judge a person. You know, first you must size up the appearance and size of the breast. Then you must watch very carefully how she eats her dinner. A movie is like a person. Either you trust it or you don't. That's all. You're not going to watch the person very carefully and say, "Well, I liked her very much until the last course. But then, frankly, I thought the way she handled her silverware was influenced by Sue." I'll tell you one thing. Agnes Varda (the French director) and I were sort of friends. We met a few times and we liked each other a lot. Then I saw one of her pictures and I thought certain things about it but I thought, Well, she knows what she is doing and I like her and that's that. Then she did a public interview about The Film—about Films, you know, that religious way that French people have—and she put down *The Graduate*. Which was fine with me. You know, anybody can put it down and I'm best of all at putting it down. But what I kept thinking was, Does she *really literally* think that films are more important than friendship? What an odd way to think. I mean, if you're going to make a religion of something, why make it of films when there are better things to make it of? And therefore I agree with you about books about film criticism.

Q: Most of the articles written about you say you had a lonely childhood.

NICHOLS: Lonely? No.

Q: Was it a happy one?

NICHOLS: Not particularly.

Q: I remember reading that after you came here from Germany, you went to the Cherry Lawn School and someone held your head under water.

NICHOLS: I don't even know if I can remember it exactly, but there was this guy who, you know, as has happened to everybody in school, there are guys you fight with, and there was this one guy who held me under water and stood on my head, so that I stayed under for some ten minutes and almost drowned. Now this was when I was, I don't know, eight? nine? And unfortunately for myself and others, I have total recall. I remember almost everything. So some years later, when Elaine and I were playing at a night club, he came to see me, and he tapped me on the shoulder and said, "You don't remember me, but—" And I said, "I remember you very well. Your name is so-and-so and you are shit." And he blanched, and I said, "What are you doing now?" And he said, "I'm working in a used-car lot." And I said, "I'm very pleased." But I'll tell you something about that. I think when people do things, they do them out of a variety of motives. Let's say, arbitrarily for a minute, you can divide why people act into three motives: vengefulness, despair, and celebration. Dig? I think for a long time, mine has been vengefulness. There was an element in everything I did of I'll-get-you-you-bastards. I think it's changing now because of things that have happened to me. I don't know if I can ever achieve celebration, though.

Q: That's fascinating, because I am totally motivated by—I call it revenge, but you called it vengefulness, and it's the same thing. So is my husband, and he has a fantasy about a person named Roland Mantifle. . . .

NICHOLS: They are all named Roland Mantifle.

Q: Roland Mantifle used to grab my husband every day after school and beat him up and take away all of his baseball cards and say unprintable demeaning things. So Dan has this fantasy that he will someday pull up in front of Roland Mantifle's low-income housing project in a Maserati and knock on the door and Roland Mantifle will answer in a T-shirt carrying a beer can, and Dan will say, "I don't know if you remember me, but my name is Dan Greenburg and I'd like to show you my bank statement."

NICHOLS: You've got to keep that story in. Would you do that for me? But listen, there are two things about that. One is that, unfortunately or fortunately, when you get to that moment, revenge is not sweet, because you're overcome, to your surprise, by sympathy for the other person. You can't do it when the moment comes. And so you're left with something—I've thought about this a little bit—you're left

with something very strange. It's not possible to divide people into two categories, but if it were, I think that it's possible that there are people to whom all the good things
happen in the first part of their lives—the Kennedys are the
world's great example of this—and then, because they can't
escape this, all the terrible things happen. And then there
is the other half of us, where the not necessarily terrible but
the pretty bad things happen in the first part, and then
things get better and they get better and then they're great.
There is only one drawback, and that is that one is poisoned
forever by the bad things that happened in the beginning. So
that if one had a choice, I think, one would choose to be the
first kind: they are the lucky ones, because they get to experience the untainted good half. Otherwise, although you can
fight it and overcome it and make something joyful and
pleasurable out of your life, there is always some poison left
from before. And you never get rid of it.

Q: You seem to have gone to about ten schools.

NICHOLS: Well, not really.

Q: Why so many?

NICHOLS: Well, we got to the United States and I went to
Dalton. I forget why. And then I didn't and I forget why.
Then I went to P.S. 87, where Mrs. Bullock used to come
into the boys' room to make sure we weren't spending too
much time in there and pull us out with her long red nails.
Then I went to Cherry Lawn, which was a postprogressive
co-educational boarding school, where you slept on sleeping
porches in the winter, with screens instead of windows and
no heat. That was to toughen your character. In my case, it
didn't work. Then I went to Walden, which was very pro-

gressive. They took us on trips ostensibly to see things like Williamsburg but really to encourage sexual intercourse as early as possible. And they were very liberated. They were liberated before anyone. The motto was "Black and white, shoulder to shoulder, against the lower class." We were all good liberals. You weren't meant to actually *work* or *learn* anything—it was much more important to be a member of your peer group. For instance, I was skipped several times in order to be a member of my peer group, and, as a result, I never had geography or penmanship. I literally do not know anything whatever about geography or penmanship, and I'm always having arguments with my girl about whether Asia is in Africa, whether Egypt is in Asia, or whether they're all separate continents. And she explains and then I forget again. I also skipped penmanship, with the very awkward result that I can't write with my hand. I can sign my name and I can write things that *I* can read and I can print when I print a note to someone, but I can't write anything that anyone else can read.

Q: What were you like at the age of sixteen?

NICHOLS: Let me think. It was my first year of college. I got out of high school at the age of fifteen and I registered at NYU. I hadn't taken the College Board exams, somehow, which made me eligible for, I believe, three schools: NYU, Mexico City College, and the University of Chicago. I opted for NYU because I was in New York. And I went there for one day. I was very self-conscious and sort of awkward and they made us stand and sing the NYU school song, which was called "Oh Grim, Gray Palisades," and I left. I went home and took a job for a year as a shipping clerk at a costume jeweler's. Then I got bored with that and tried out for

Mexico City College and Chicago. I was accepted at Chicago and went there and that was when I was sixteen and it was a very very happy year for me. It was sort of—and I think I've said this before—it was the first time I realized that life wasn't frozen in that high-school pattern forever. You know, in high school you think, Mike Tenzer can beat me up and I can beat up Dave Halpern. And Laura Lichtenstein will go out with me and Lenore Firestein will *never*. And life will be like this *forever*. Do you remember that?

Q: Oh, God, yes.

NICHOLS: And I got to college and I thought, Jesus, the world is full of possibilities. And the world is not frozen and I am not frozen. And I was very happy at sixteen.

Q: But you soon dropped out of school.

NICHOLS: Yes. I don't know if you know about the Hutchins system (after Robert M. Hutchins, former president of the University of Chicago), but at the time, when I went to Chicago, you first took a placement exam, and if you knew something, you didn't have to study it. You took a test where you mark the paper and the machine decides if you're right. Well, later on they caught this and it was no longer possible, but there was one girl who didn't understand any of the biology questions, so she drew a duck, using the little spaces, with her electromagnetic pencil, and she got a B. I placed out of math and physics, which I knew nothing about, through luck. Anyway, then they tell you what you have to study and you don't have to go to class. So, of course I never did go. I sort of hung around and talked to people and drank and sometimes read the texts and sometimes didn't, and at the end of the year you take a comprehensive exam. Which I did and sort of got through the first year. But then the next year the whole thing began to disintegrate. I hadn't gone to class and I enjoyed my friends and drinking and living more and more, so I ended up not taking the comprehensive exams either. And then I wasn't in school any more. But there were lots of us like that and we just sort of lived in Chicago, and it was a terrific community and a very happy time. We all lived in the same neighborhood, and you came out of your house and ran into your friends and had breakfast in the drugstore, and the theater that we formed began to come out of that. I'd known Elaine, but then something happened between us that led to many things—to the theater and the cabaret and so on.

Q: I read that you were very depressed after you broke up the act with Elaine May. What was that period like?

NICHOLS: It was like hell. I was the leftover half of something—both professionally and otherwise. I didn't know what the point of me was, or what I was supposed to do next. So I bummed around and felt sorry for myself and was a pain in the ass to my friends and complained a lot and did dopey things like acting on TV shows and directing at the Vancouver Festival—oh, and acting in it. I was the Dauphin in *Saint Joan* opposite Susan Kohner.

Q: No kidding.

NICHOLS: Yes. I played the Dauphin to her Joan. One night while she was giving us her Joan, I knocked one of her teeth out. By mistake, needless to say. That wasn't a success in any way. Also it was in Vancouver, and if you haven't been in Vancouver, it's very hard to describe. But I also would have fits in the middle of rehearsal where I would fall on the floor and start screaming, "I'm in Canada. I'm in Canada." And they would all just stare at me. And then I would have temper tantrums, and once I said, "Blow it up. We'll get our ginger ale somewhere else." I hated it. And then Saint Subber (the Broadway producer) thought maybe I could direct a play. He offered me *Barefoot in the Park*, and I thought, Let's try.

Q: I wondered if you had anything to say about improvisation as training for acting or for life.

NICHOLS: As training for acting, I think it makes you very comfortable with the audience and it makes you think, I can take care of you guys. Don't worry. But what I really thought it was useful for was directing, because it also teaches you what a scene is made of—you know, what needs to happen. See, I think the audience asks the question, "Why are you telling me this?" And improvisation teaches you that you *must* answer it. There must be a specific answer. It also teaches you when the beginning is over and it's time for the middle, and when you've had enough middle and it's time already for the end. And those are all very useful things in directing.

Q: And what about as training for life?

NICHOLS: Nothing trains you for life.

On Location With
Catch-22

March 1969

It is a moment of intense concentration. Mike Nichols is sitting in a blue director's chair, his face contorted, his hands clenched, his eyes squeezed shut. He finally opens his mouth to speak. "Bladder," he says. "Whimsy. Dailies. Rumble. Barren. Crystal. Pastry."

"No," says Tony Perkins, who is seated next to him. "Not pastry."

"Strudel," says Nichols triumphantly. "Strudel. Pepsi. Cancer. Stopwatch. . . ."

A film is being shot here. Not at the moment, of course. At the moment, the director of the film is playing a memory game with one of the actors while the crew figures out how to work a broken water machine that is holding up the shooting. The name of the film is *Catch-22*. It is budgeted at eleven million dollars, is on location in the Mexican desert, and is based on Joseph Heller's best-selling World War Two novel. "I've tried, as they say, to preserve the integrity of the novel," says screenwriter Buck Henry. "Don't print that unless you put after it: 'He said this with a glint in his eye and a twitch in his cheek and a kick in the groin.' Because if that line so much as looks as if I said it seriously, I'll kill you." Among the graffiti scrawled on the wall of the portable men's room on the set is one that reads, HELP SAVE JOE HELLER.

A film is being shot here—between memory games, word games, repartee, kibitzing, and general good cheer. *Catch-22*, the story of Captain John Yossarian and his ultimate refusal to fly any more bombing missions. The movie of the year. A film actors signed up for before they knew what parts they were playing or how much money they would get for their work. With Alan Arkin starring as Yossarian, and Orson Welles (General Dreedle), Martin Balsam (Colonel Cathcart), Dick Benjamin (Major Danby), Norman Fell (Sergeant Towser), Jack Gilford (Doc Daneeka), Tony Perkins (Chaplain Tappman), and Paula Prentiss (Nurse Duckett). Art Garfunkel, of Simon and Garfunkel, will make his acting debut as Captain Nately. "What I feel like here," said Seth Allen, a young actor in the film, "is a near great."

Whether *Catch-22* will be a masterpiece, merely a very funny film, or the first failure for Mike Nichols after those two smash-hit movies and seven hit plays is at this point almost an irrelevant question for the actors in it. What matters is that the film is a chance to work with Nichols, who, at thirty-seven, is the most successful director in America and probably the most popular actor's director in the world.

Says Orson Welles, "Nobody's in his league with actors." What's more, he is the one of a handful of American directors since Welles made *Citizen Kane* in 1941 who have had complete creative control over the final product—including the contractual right of final cut and the option of not showing his rushes to studio executives.

Nichols is too modest and far too intelligent not to realize the absurdity of being in this position after making two films and directing for only seven years. "Every time you get too much for what you've put in," he said, "you know it's going to come out of your ass later." But, for now, he is going about his business—wandering about the set, in stylish fatigue jacket and slender corduroy pants; offering Oreos and Oh Henrys to the crew; bringing his low-key techniques to his actors' assistance; and somehow managing to keep his macroproduction company happy and on schedule. *Catch-22* is to shoot in Mexico for four months, move to Los Angeles for four weeks of airplane-interior shots, and then to Rome until mid-June. After ten months of editing, it will be ready for release in mid-1970.

It has taken eight years to bring Heller's book to the shooting stage. In the interim, the novel, after a slow beginning and mixed reviews, has become a modern classic, with a Modern Library edition and two million paperback copies in print. The film property has passed from Columbia to Paramount/Filmways, from Richard Brooks (who did little or nothing with it for four years) to Mike Nichols, from Jack Lemmon (who originally wanted to play Yossarian) to Arkin, and from one unsuccessful treatment by Richard Quine to four drafts by Henry (whose previous film credits include *The Graduate* and *Candy*). It took Nichols, producer John Calley, and designer Richard Sylbert over a year just to find the ideal spot to build the island of Pianosa and its air base—largely because the logical locations in Italy, Sicily, Sardinia, and Corsica no longer look like Italy, Sicily, Sardinia, and Corsica did in 1944.

Casting began, with Nichols selecting a group of actors, all of whom look like ordinary people, to play fighter pilots, and with Frank Tallman, the stunt pilot, rounding up a group of authentic fighter pilots, all of whom look like movie stars, to fly the planes. Tallman also set to work locating and assembling a squadron of B-25s—eighteen of them, each purchased, repaired, and made skyworthy at an average cost of ten thousand dollars. (One of the planes, a wedding present from heiress Barbara Hutton to playboy Porfirio Rubirosa, came complete with reclining seats, bed, and leather-paneled toilet.)

Sylbert and Calley finally found the location on the northwest coast of Mexico, twenty miles from the town of Guaymas, Sonora, the home of Guaymas shrimp and little else. The location was a flawless one photographically—with ocean flanking it on one side and mountains set just two miles behind—but it was reachable only by boat. It cost one hundred eighty thousand dollars to build the five-mile-long highway to the spot, and two hundred fifty thousand more for the six-thousand-foot-long runway. Both construction jobs were undertaken, ecstatically, by the mayor of Guaymas, who just happens to own a contracting company. Seventy-five *peones* working with machetes cleared the one-mile-square site of cactus, brush, and rattlesnakes, leaving only mesquite trees, which resembled the small olive trees native to Italy. And Pianosa rose from the sand, with its tents, corrugated tin huts, mess hall, control tower, lister-bag setups, and piles of bombs stacked like supermar-

ket oranges along the runway. War-beaten stone buildings
were designed with collapsible walls, in preparation for the
moment in *Catch-22* when Milo Minderbinder (played by
Jon Voight), leads the men in a bombing raid on their own
base.

The most critical problem Nichols and Henry faced in
translating the book to cinematic terms was in finding a
style for Heller's macabre comedy. "The book, and, as a result, the film, have to be somewhat dreamlike, not quite
real—either something remembered, or a nightmare," said
Nichols. "That's very hard to do with living actors, with
pores and noses, because they're so definitely there. If you're
making a film in which an officer says, 'You mean the en-
listed men pray to the same God that we do?' and in which
the men bomb their own base, you have to find a style that
makes it clear, from the beginning, that such things can
happen."

The solution was to make the story arise from a fever
Yossarian develops after being stabbed in the side by
Nately's whore; the film leaps back and forth from vaguely-
remembered-horror to farce to better-remembered-horror.
"The picture will be cut as if Yossarian's delirium were cutting it," Henry explained. The style has been further carried
out in the set—which has a ghostly quality—and in Nichols'
decision to send home two hundred extras after the first
week of shooting, leaving only Yossarian and his friends to
fill out the huge air base. In addition, David Watkin, the
English cinematographer who shot the Richard Lester
Beatles films, has lit *Catch-22* so that all the actors are in
shadow and the background is burned out; the effect is of a
subliminal limbo.

Like the novel, the film hangs on the notion of Catch-22,

a masterpiece of muddled military logic. "Let me get this straight," says Yossarian to Doc Daneeka in the script. "In order to be grounded I have to be crazy. And I must be crazy to keep flying. But if I ask to be grounded—that means I'm not crazy any more and I have to keep flying."

"You got it," says Doc Daneeka. "That's Catch-22."

As a multitude of reporters and critics have observed since the book was published in October 1961, *Catch-22* has almost become a primer for the thinking that has seemed to be guiding the war in Vietnam. At the same time, the predicament of Yossarian has become more relevant in the context of the antiwar movement in this country. "The interesting thing about the book," said Buck Henry, who despite his disclaimer has been quite faithful to the novel, "is the enormous power of prophecy Heller had. He was writing about a man who had finally decided to opt out and who in the end ends up in Sweden. That was a total absurdity when he wrote it, a really far-out kind of insanity. Well, it's come true."

That *Catch-22* is being made in an atmosphere of such good feeling is as much a part of the Nichols approach as any of the directing techniques he utilizes. "If you're on the set shooting," Nichols explained, "and you say, 'Let's do it again,' and there's one guy who rolls his eyes or turns away or groans, it sours it for everybody. John and Buck and I said, 'Let's see if for once we can have nobody like that—just people who like each other.' And it worked." Many of the cast members are old friends and about half have worked with Nichols before. They have been laughing ever since a chartered jet brought them from Los Angeles to Mexico on January 2 and landed them smack in the middle of the utterly barren, desolate desert. "Look at this," Bob Newhart said, as he stepped out of the plane. Everyone looked around at what looked like the end of the world. "Ten years ago I could have bought land here," said Newhart, "and look at it now."

When the film is between takes, the cast sits around and roars with laughter as Bob Newhart spins out a routine on night life in Guaymas (there is none) or Buck Henry and Tony Perkins improvise on the subject of free falling and parachute jumping:

Perkins: "What about all this we hear about the free-fall mass?"

Henry: "There are two free-fall masses."

Perkins: "The eleven o'clock and the seven o'clock?"

Henry: "No. In the fall of 1965 a town of thirteen hundred people in Nevada went up and made a fall."

Perkins: "I was speaking of the free-fall mass, not the mass free fall."

Henry: "The free-fall mass is where the falling priest throws the wafer and the parishioners jump out of the plane and dive for it. It's called diving for the wafer. That's where the expression comes from. Dive for the wafer, dig for the wine."

Perkins: "What about this lady who jumped with her cats?"

Henry: "Well, actually, that story was not reported accurately. There was a lady, but she jumped with her lawyer, whose name was Katz."

When the film is shooting, the director and crew stand behind the camera, biting their lips and gritting their teeth to keep from exploding with laughter during the take.

Nichols' snorts of appreciation affect the actors in about the same way the bowl of food did Pavlov's dogs. "I'm so overjoyed when he laughs," said Paula Prentiss, "that I don't even care that half the time I don't know what he's laughing at."

"You never get hung up if Mike is directing you," said Miss Prentiss's husband, Dick Benjamin. "If you're doing a scene you're not comfortable with, he senses it, and before it can get to be a problem for you, he gives you two or three specific things to do—like a piece of business or a new line or something. And you think, Oh, I get to do *that*. Like a kid who's been given a birthday present. Everything else sort of falls into place and you get your little goodies. And Mike talks in terms of that. He'll say, 'I've really got a present for so-and-so when he gets to Rome.' And he means he's got some wonderful shot, something to do, some way the actor will look that is just sensational. And you really take it as a present."

Sometimes Nichols will give an actor a short suggestion or line reading that will suddenly clarify the role. To Benjamin, who was playing a scene in which he was supposed to be terrified of Orson Welles' General Dreedle, Nichols—who was himself terrified of Orson Welles—said simply, "Watch me." To Austin Pendleton, who was confused as to how to play Welles' son-in-law, Colonel Moodus, Nichols gave a line reading that, said Pendleton, "gave me the key to the whole thing. I realized he wanted me to play the kind of person who says the most insulting things as if he's being terribly friendly." To Norman Fell, Nichols suggested playing Sergeant Towser as a military mammy; as a result, Fell delivers the most blood-curdling lines with a funny little smile on his face, as if he were talking about chicken and gravy and wonderful biscuits.

Occasionally, Nichols will add an especially intimate gift to the proceedings. One morning he was shooting a close-up of Buck Henry (who also appears in the film, as Colonel Korn) and Martin Balsam (Colonel Cathcart). Henry was to lean over and whisper to Balsam, "He's talking to you." Balsam was to pop to attention and deliver an answer. Nichols shot two takes of the scene and then called Henry over for a conference. "Let's do another," he said. Henry returned to position and the scene began again. "He's talking to you!" hissed Henry, and he leaned over and goosed Balsam. Balsam jumped, his eyes bugged out of his head, and he managed to deliver his line before losing his composure. The crew broke up. "Nichols Directs," said Henry, "—a Monograph on the Unusual Techniques of a Young American Director: 'Use three fingers,' he said to me."

On another occasion, Nichols was shooting a love scene between Arkin and Miss Prentiss (Nurse Duckett). The footage—of Yossarian's hand sliding up Duckett's leg—was fine, but Nichols had not been able to get the right vocal reaction from the actress. He called a take for sound only. And as Arkin began to slip his hand up Miss Prentiss's skirt, Nichols grabbed her from behind and plunked his hands onto her breasts. "I let out this great hoot," said Miss Prentiss, "which Mike was very happy with. Then I was so overcome with emotion I had to go into a corner and be alone. Whenever someone touches me I'm in love with him for about eight hours."

"It's perfectly possible," Nichols conceded, "that we can have this great time now, making the film, and then have it not be a good picture. The two have nothing to do with each other. But then, none of us knows whether the picture is any good even long after it's finished, so you might as well be happy while it's going on. And when the actors break up and the crew is stuffing handkerchiefs into their mouths trying not to laugh at Dick Benjamin—or whoever it is—I love it. I love it now. Afterward, it's up for grabs anyway."

For the actors, at least, making an air-force film has turned out to be very much like being in the air force. Not when they are working: when they work, making *Catch-22* is like being at a party, a festival, a love-in. But because so many of the actors have small parts, they have a great deal of time to kill in a town where there is almost nothing to do. As a result, many of them spend their empty days discussing how many days of shooting each has to go. When they tire of kicking that subject around, they move on to other tried-and-true service talk. "I'll tell you what we do around here in our free time," said Alan Arkin. "We sit in the barracks out at the set with our muddy boots on and talk about women. That's what you do in the army, isn't it? Sit around in your muddy boots and talk about women? I don't know why we do it. Almost everyone here is with his wife or his girl friend. But that's what we do."

They complain about the food in the mess hall—that is, the mess hall on the set, which doubles as a lunch commissary complete with regulation army trays. They complain about the living accommodations at the Playa de Cortès, Guaymas's somewhat unsatisfactory attempt at a luxury hotel. They complain about their isolation from the outside world. And they complain about the incredible difficulty of obtaining newspapers and placing long-distance calls. "We make bets on who's going to go insane," says Bob Newhart, "or has already gone insane. In fact, maybe we've all gone insane and we're all together and we don't know it and we'll go home and my wife will call Paramount and say, 'Listen, my husband is insane.' We have no norm here. We have no way of judging."

That everyone in this squadron of professed lunatics is good-natured, noncompetitive, and thoroughly professional is small consolation. By February, several of the cast members had begun to complain that the company was *too* nice. "If only there were a lemon here," said Tony Perkins. "It would give us something to talk about."

Any location—outside of London, Paris, and Rome—is bound to breed complaint; but the actors, who seem to be playing a private game of Kvetch-22, have hardly been on a dull movie. Within the first two weeks of shooting, a case of hepatitis broke out, requiring that the entire company be inoculated. A B-25, caught in propwash, nearly crashed into the control tower while shooting was going on. Susanne Benton, a starlet who plays General Dreedle's WAC, complete with seven pairs of falsies and a rubber behind by Frederick's of Hollywood, was accidentally clobbered by a camera during a take and passed out cold. Two actors, mistakenly released for a short trip to New York, were headed off on the way to the airport by a hastily dispatched helicopter, which landed, à la James Bond, ahead of them on the highway. There was even an unexpected, action-packed visit from John Wayne—though reports differ as to exactly what happened during it.

According to consensus, Wayne, on his way to make a Western in Durango, radioed the field for permission to land his plane. Permission was granted. When Wayne arrived, producer Calley met him and asked if he would like to see the shooting, which was going on in a tent some distance away. No, Wayne said, he wanted to drive to a part of the location to see some land he was thinking of buying. But some time later, he showed up at the shooting. He stood around, apparently waiting for a welcoming party; but none of the actors knew him, and Nichols and Henry did not emerge to greet him. Wayne went to the Playa de Cortès and spent the evening in the bar, drinking, smashing glassware, and complaining that he had been snubbed—possibly for political reasons. Ultimately, he fell and broke a couple of ribs.

"We didn't snub him at all," Henry said later. "We were in the tent, and for some undiscernible dumb reason, no one said, 'Come on out and meet the big guy.' We're trying to make up for it by getting a print of *The Green Berets* and showing it to the crew. In the meantime, we've just been sitting around here, watching the days go by, and waiting for him to come back and bomb us."

The arrival of Orson Welles, for two weeks of shooting in February, was just the therapy the company needed: at the very least, it gave everyone something to talk about. The situation was almost melodramatically ironic: Welles, the great American director now unable to obtain big-money backing for his films, was being directed by thirty-seven-year-old Nichols; Welles, who had tried, unsuccessfully, to buy *Catch-22* for himself in 1962, was appearing in it to pay for his new film *Dead Reckoning*. The cast spent days preparing for his arrival. *Touch of Evil* was flown in and microscopically viewed. *Citizen Kane* was discussed over dinner. Tony Perkins, who had appeared in Welles' *The Trial*, was repeatedly asked What Orson Welles Was Really Like. Bob Balaban, a young actor who plays Orr in the film, laid plans to retrieve one of Welles' cigar butts for an admiring friend.

303-465-2286 • Fax 303-465-1122 • Toll Free 877-465-2286
info@summitrecreation.com
www.summitrecreation.com

And Nichols began to combat his panic by imagining what it would be like to direct a man of Welles' stature.

"Before he came," said Nichols, "I had two fantasies. The first was that he would say his first line, and I would say, 'NO, NO, NO, Orson!' " He laughed. "Then I thought perhaps not. The second was that he would arrive on the set and I would say, 'Mr. Welles, now if you'd be so kind as to move over here. . . .' And he'd look at me and raise one eyebrow and say, 'Over there?' And I'd say, 'What? Oh, uh, where do *you* think it should be?' "

Welles landed in Guaymas with an entourage that included a cook and film maker Peter Bogdanovich, who was interviewing him for a Truffaut-Hitchcock type memoir. For the eight days it took to shoot his two scenes, he dominated the set. He stood on the runway, his huge wet Havana cigar tilting just below his squinting eyes and sagging eye pouches, addressing Nichols and the assembled cast and crew. Day after day he told fascinating stories of dubbing in Bavaria, looping in Italy, and shooting in Yugoslavia. He also told Nichols how to direct the film, the crew how to move the camera, film editor Sam O'Steen how to cut a scene, and most of the actors how to deliver their lines. Welles even lectured Martin Balsam for three minutes on how to deliver the line, "Yes, sir."

A few of the actors did not mind at all. Austin Pendleton, who plays Welles' son-in-law, got along with Welles simply by talking back to him.

"Are you sure you wouldn't like to say that line more slowly?" Welles asked Pendleton one day.

"Yes," Pendleton replied slowly. "I am sure."

But after a few days of shooting, many of the other actors were barely concealing their hostility toward Welles—

particularly because of his tendency to blow his lines during takes. By the last day of shooting, when Welles used his own procedure, a lengthy and painstaking one, to shoot a series of closeups, most of the people on the set had managed to tune out on the big, booming raconteur.

But Mike Nichols managed to glide through the two-week siege without showing a trace of irritation with Welles. And whenever the famous Welles eyebrow rose after one of Nichols' camera decisions, Nichols would turn to him and smile and say, "No good, huh? Where should it go?"

"Mike controlled the Welles thing simply by respecting Welles," said Austin Pendleton. "After all, if there's any one person who has a right to say where a cut should be made, it's Orson. Mike respected that. And Orson knew it."

At the same time, Nichols carefully smoothed the ruffled feathers among his company. And he got a magnificent performance, from Welles as well as from the rest of the cast. "The Welles situation, which brought a lot of people down, was almost identical to the tension that was written in the script," said Peter Bonerz, a young West Coast actor who plays McWatt in the film. "We were all under the thumb of this huge, cigar-smoking general, as written, and at the same time, we were under the thumb of this huge, cigar-smoking director. The discomfort that we were feeling was real, and I'm sure it looks grand on film."

One day shortly after Welles had left (taking with him his general's uniform, which he wore around Guaymas for two days until a costume man was able to retrieve it), Nichols sat in his trailer on the set. Outside, it was hot, dusty, and windy. But the trailer was air conditioned, with an icebox full of brownies imported from Greenberg's bakery in New York, and Nichols sat eating one and talking about himself, his success, and the Welles episode:

"What I wanted to say to Welles was this—I wanted to say, '*I* know you're Orson Welles, and *I* know I'm *me*. I never *said* I was Mike Nichols. Those *other* people said that.' What I mean by that is that he's a great man. I know he's a great man. I never said I was. And, of course, you can't say such things.

"We were talking about [Jean] Renoir one day on the set, and Orson said, very touchingly, that Renoir was a great man but that, unfortunately, Renoir didn't like his pictures. And then he said, 'Of course, if I were Renoir, I wouldn't like my pictures either.' And I wanted to say to him, 'If I were Orson Welles, I wouldn't like *my* pictures either, and it's O.K., and I agree with you, and what can I do?'

"I never said all that stuff about me. I'm not happy about this thing that's building up about me, because it has nothing to do with me. I mean, the things I've done are neither as good as the people who carry on say they are, nor are they as bad as the reaction to the reaction says they are. They're just sort of in-between. I'm not flagellating myself and saying I've turned out only crap, because I'm not ashamed of it and some of it I like very much. But Orson said to somebody that he didn't just want to be a festival director." He paused. "Well, I guess if you have the festivals and *Cahiers* and Pauline Kael and Andrew Sarris, you want to make pictures that break box-office records. And it also works the other way around.

"I was very moved by Welles. I knew what it felt like to be him in that situation, to come into a company in the middle, to have a tremendous reputation not to like acting, to be used to being in control—and I was sorry when people didn't see what that felt like. Where the camera is and what it does is so much a part of his life—how is he suddenly supposed to ignore it? Take somebody like Elizabeth Taylor—when she's acting, she knows where the light is and how close the shot is. Orson knows whether he's in focus or not. Literally. If you know that much, what are you supposed to do with it? You can't throw it out. And I know that if I were acting in a movie, it would be very hard for me not to say, 'I wonder if you would be kind enough to consider putting the camera a little more there so that when I do this . . .' How do you kill that knowledge?"

Nichols stopped, lit a Parliament from a stack of cigarette packs on the trailer table, and began to talk about what the Beatles used to call The Fall. "I almost can't wait for it to come," he said. "Because I'm somewhat upset by the Midas bullshit and also by the reaction to the Midas bullshit. I don't like a critic to tell me that I set out to make a success, because it's not true. There's enough worry in thinking that you set out to do the very best you could and came out with only a success—that's depressing about oneself. You know, none of the great movies has been a popular success. I can't think of any exceptions. But you accept that there's a great difference between yourself and the artists who make films. It's like when you're fourteen years old and you realize that Tchaikovsky would have liked to be Mozart—he just didn't have a choice. And I'm not even making a comparison there. But you have to go on as yourself. I'd like to be better, but I can't."

From outside the trailer came a knock, and a voice said, "Mr. Nichols, we're ready for you now." The water machine was working. The actors were on the set. And Nichols hopped out of the air-conditioned vehicle into the heat and began to walk over to the stone building where the cameras were set up. A few feet away, Buck Henry was having difficulty with a crossword puzzle. "Are there any Hindus here?" he was shouting. "One of your festivals is bothering me." A film is being shot here.

About the Author

NORA EPHRON is also the author of *I Feel Bad About My Neck*, *Crazy Salad*, *Scribble Scribble*, and *Heartburn*. She received Academy Award nominations for Best Original Screenplay for *When Harry Met Sally . . .* , *Silkwood*, and *Sleepless in Seattle*, which she also directed. Her other credits include the films *Michael* and *You've Got Mail*, and the play *Imaginary Friends*. She lives in New York City with her husband, writer Nicholas Pileggi.